THE BOSS-LADY

Borgo Press Books Edited & Translated by FRANK J. MORLOCK

Alcestis: A Play in Five Acts, by Philippe Quinault * *Anna Karenina: A Play in Five Acts*, by Edmond Guiraud, from Leo Tolstoy * *Anthony: A Play in Five Acts*, by Alexandre Dumas, Père * *Atys: A Play in Five Acts*, by Philippe Quinault * *The Boss-Lady: A Play in Five Acts*, by Paul Féval, Père * *The Children of Captain Grant: A Play in Five Acts*, by Jules Verne & Adolphe d'Ennery * *Cleopatra: A Play in Five Acts*, by Victorien Sardou * *Crime and Punishment: A Play in Three Acts*, by Frank J. Morlock, from Fyodor Dostoyevsky * *Don Quixote: A Play in Three Acts*, by Victorien Sardou, from Miguel de Cervantes * *The Dream of a Summer Night: A Fantasy Play in Three Acts*, by Paul Meurice * *Falstaff: A Play in Four Acts*, by William Shakespeare, John Dennis, William Kendrick, & Frank J. Morlock * *The Idiot: A Play in Three Acts*, by Frank J. Morlock, from Fyodor Dostoyevsky * *Isis: A Play in Five Acts*, by Philippe Quinault * *Jesus of Nazareth: A Play in Three Acts*, by Paul Demasy * *The Jew of Venice: A Play in Five Acts*, by Ferdinand Dugué * *Joan of Arc: A Play in Five Acts*, by Charles Desnoyer * *The Lily of the Valley: A Play in Five Acts*, by Théodore Barrière & Arthur de Beauplan, from Honoré de Balzac * *Lord Byron in Venice: A Play in Three Acts*, by Jacques Ancelot * *Louis XIV and the Affair of the Poisons: A Play in Five Acts*, by Victorien Sardou * *The Man Who Saw the Devil: A Play in Two Acts*, by Gaston Leroux * *Mathias Sandorf: A Play in Three Acts*, by Jules Verne & William Busnach * *Michael Strogoff: A Play in Five Acts*, by Jules Verne & Adolphe d'Ennery * *Les Misérables: A Play in Two Acts*, by Victor Hugo, Paul Meurice, & Charles Victor Hugo * *Monte Cristo, Part One: A Play in Five Acts*, by Alexandre Dumas, Père * *Monte Cristo, Part Two: A Play in Five Acts*, by Alexandre Dumas, Père * *Monte Cristo, Part Three: A Play in Five Acts*, by Alexandre Dumas, Père * *Monte Cristo, Part Four: A Play in Five Acts*, by Alexandre Dumas, Père * *The Musketeers: A Play in Five Acts*, by Alexandre Dumas, Père * *The Mysteries of Paris: A Play in Five Acts*, by Eugène Sue & Prosper Dinaux * *Napoléon Bonaparte: A Play in Six Acts*, by Alexandre Dumas, Père * *Ninety-Three: A Play in Four Acts*, by Victor Hugo & Paul Meurice * *Notes from the Underground: A Play in Two Acts*, by Frank J. Morlock, from Fyodor Dostoyevsky * *Outrageous Women: Lady MacBeth and Other French Plays*, edited by Frank J. Morlock * *Peau de Chagrin: A Play in Five Acts*, by Louis Judicis, from Honoré de Balzac * *The Prisoner of the Bastille: A Play in Five Acts*, by Alexandre Dumas, Père * *A Raw Youth: A Play in Five Acts*, by Frank J. Morlock, from Fyodor Dostoyevsky * *Richard Darlington: A Play in Three Acts*, by Alexandre Dumas, Père * *The San Felice: A Play in Five Acts*, by Maurice Drack, from Alexander Dumas, Père * *Saul and David: A Play in Five Acts*, by Voltaire * *Shylock, the Merchant of Venice: A Play in Three Acts*, by Alfred de Vigny * *Socrates: A Play in Three Acts*, by Voltaire * *The Son of Porthos: A Play in Five Acts*, by Émile Blavet, from M. Paul Mahalin * *The Stendhal Hamlet Scenarios and Other Shakespearean Shorts from the French*, edited by Frank J. Morlock * *A Summer Night's Dream: A Play in Three Acts*, by Joseph-Bernard Rosier & Adolphe de Leuwen * *The Three Musketeers: A Play in Five Acts*, by Alexandre Dumas, Père * *Urbain Grandier and the Devils of Loudon: A Play in Four Acts*, by Alexandre Dumas, Père * *The Voyage Through the Impossible: A Play in Three Acts*, by Jules Verne & Adolphe d'Ennery * *The Whites and the Blues: A Play in Five Acts*, by Alexandre Dumas, Père * *William Shakespeare: A Play in Six Acts*, by Ferdinand Dugué

THE BOSS-LADY

A Play in Five Acts

by

Paul Féval, Père

Translated and Adapted by Frank J. Morlock

The Borgo Press

An Imprint of Wildside Press LLC

MMX

Copyright © 2008, 2010 by Frank J. Morlock

All rights reserved. No part of this book may be reproduced without the expressed written consent of the author. Professionals are warned that this material, being fully protected under the copyright laws of the United States of America, and all other countries of the Berne and Universal Copyright Convention, is subject to a royalty. All rights, including all forms of performance now existing or later invented, but not limited to professional, amateur, recording, motion picture, recitation, public reading, radio, television broadcasting, DVD, and Role Playing Games, and all rights of translation into foreign languages, are expressly reserved. Particular emphasis is placed on the question of readings, and all uses of these plays by educational institutions, permission for which must be secured in advance from the author's publisher, Wildside Press, 9710 Traville Gateway Dr. #234, Rockville, MD 20850 (phone 301-762-1305).

www.wildsidebooks.com

FIRST WILDSIDE EDITION

CONTENTS

Cast of Characters 7

Act I 9

Act II 46

Act III 78

Act IV 108

Act V 145

About the Editor 178

DEDICATION

TO

GABRIELLE, MY BOSS-LADY

CAST OF CHARACTERS

Prince STANISLAS Leszczynski, son of King Stanislas I of Poland

Chevalier ANDRÉ de Rieux

BONAVENTURE, waiter at the Inn

CHAMPAGNE

CORNIL VAN ZUYP

ROBIN

MOREL

FRANÇOIS Picot

The BAILIFF of Quilleboeuf

JOLIBOIS, postillon

BOUTE-ENTRAIN, postillon

An INNKEEPER (feminine)

ROSALIE Valentin, the Boss-Lady

Frau VAN ZUYP, VAN ZUYP's wife

MINON, adoptive sister of ROSALIE

THÉRÈSE

A COUTURIER

Waiters, Workers, Postillons, etc.

ACT I

The Inn of the White Horse.

A smoky Inn in Lorraine in a dark and country style. Three doors with a usable window. A bed with a trunk in front of it.

BONAVENTURE: (Off)

Fine. I'm going to do my work, Boss-Lady.

(Comes in)

She told me to be gay. Each is gay in his way! My word, when I'm in a good mood I feel like crying.

(Drying his eyes)

MINON: (Curling her hair in front of a mirror)

They're going to dance. What happiness!

BONAVENTURE: (Sadly)

Ah, yes, just what I was saying. What happiness.

MINON:

My sister Rosalie will be really happy with François Picot.

BONAVENTURE: (Heatedly)

If she were not happy—?

MINON: (Taking up her work)

François Picot is a good lad.

BONAVENTURE:

Not good enough for Madame Rosalie!

MINON:

If she chose him for her husband it's 'cause she loves him.

BONAVENTURE: (Sadly)

Ah, yes. She must have loved him to have chosen him.

MINON:

After all, the White Horse Inn cannot go without a man, can it? Old man Valentin never gets out of his bed, my sister Rosalie needs someone to impose on the costumers—now especially with so many folks of bad appearance coming—because of the State Prisoner who's in the Château.

BONAVENTURE: (Sighing)

Ah, yes. There must be a man for this woman.

MINON:

And how nice the engagement's going to be.—Have you seen engagements before, Bonaventure?—At midnight a beautiful party (dreamily) that lasts until dawn.

Ah, it's really nice to get married.

BONAVENTURE: (Sighing)

Ah, yes!

(Aside) With Madame Rosalie, especially.

(Aloud) Hold on, Miss Minon—if this François Picot wasn't a good husband—because, you see—he will have an angel for a wife.

MINON:

Poor Bonaventure! Rosalie will still scold you sometimes.

BONAVENTURE:

That signifies nothing. I prefer to be scolded by Madame Rosalie than to be caressed by someone else.

(Aside, with terror) Gossip! You talk too much.

MINON: (At the window)

Here's the brown-haired one coming. In a few hours they'll be fiancés.

BONAVENTURE: (Aside)

In a few hours!

(He dusts the tables with rage)

MINON: (Dreamily, aside)

Two days he hasn't come! As soon as he appears I'll get out of here. When he doesn't come, I am sad and I weep. What would you say about that, Holy Virgin?

(She shivers and sets to listen)

It's his step!

(She hurriedly grabs her sewing)

It's him! It's really him.

(ANDRÉ de Rieux enters in very simple hunting poaching costume. At the moment he appears in the doorway, MINON blushing and smiling squirms out. He seeks to detain her with a supplicating gesture, she shakes her head. He blows her a kiss; she vanishes.)

BONAVENTURE:

It's the poacher. He pleases me well enough. He's not coming for Madame Rosalie.

ANDRÉ:

No one has come to ask for me?

BONAVENTURE:

No one.

ANDRÉ:

I'll wait. What are they saying in the country?

(He sits at a table)

BONAVENTURE:

Nothing.

ANDRÉ:

So it's you, friend, and this charming child who are owners of this Inn?

BONAVENTURE:

No. It's old man Valentin and his daughter.

ANDRÉ:

I've never seen them.

BONAVENTURE:

The old man never leaves his bed—and you always come at the time, when Miss Rosalie is looking after her sick father. But you, what profession do your practice around here?

ANDRÉ:

A tough job in which I risk my skin.

BONAVENTURE:

I wouldn't like that kind of work.

ANDRÉ:

And the young girl?

BONAVENTURE: (Dryly)

She's not half so beautiful as Madame Rosalie.

(Enter ROBIN and MOREL)

ROBIN:

Something to drink.

MOREL:

And be quick about it.

BONAVENTURE: Coming.

(Leaving) Bad faces!

ROBIN:

You got here fast, Mr. André. We've had a long run.

ANDRÉ:

Have you seen the Prince?

ROBIN:

Yes, in the woods of Saint Étienne. They let him hunt, but they keep him in sight.

ANDRÉ:

Have you been able to speak to him?

ROBIN:

That requires time and skill. Finally I was able to approach him undercover and I slipped the name of André de Rieux in his ear. He shivered.

"He's my best friend," he said; "what's he want with me?" "A meeting." "Where?" "In the White Horse Inn." "When?" "At eight o'clock this evening." "I'll be there."

ANDRÉ:

Fine—you will be rewarded.

MOREL:

We're sort of dry, Mr. André.

ANDRÉ:

I'm expecting funds. At eight o'clock you'll be near this inn to spring the trap. As for me, I'm going to inform my friends.

(He leaves)

ROBIN:

Morel!

MOREL:

Robin!

ROBIN:

Always promises.

MOREL:

Always.

ROBIN:

Never any money.

MOREL:

Never.

ROBIN:

Morel, my friend, this begins to no longer suit me—this business.

MOREL:

My friend Robin, it hasn't suited me for a long while.

BONAVENTURE: (Bringing wine)

Here! Heavens, the poacher has left. That one is never thirsty.

ROBIN:

Fine—beat it!

BONAVENTURE:

I cannot continue my work.

ROBIN:

Beat it. We have to talk.

BONAVENTURE:

Those two displease me, but that's the way it goes.

(He leaves)

ROBIN:

Mr. André de Rieux! That name sounds nice.

MOREL:

His pocket sounds empty.

ROBIN: (Sticking his cap)

Like me it seems that Prince Stanislas of Poland is no longer as rich as he was.

MOREL:

Czar Peter of Russia who came last year to Paris.—Now there was a prince! Rolling in money!

ROBIN:

Yes, but Czar Peter of Russia is 500 leagues from here—and he has no need of us.

CHAMPAGNE: (Who has quietly entered)

No need to swear, comrades—

(MOREL and ROBIN rise precipitously)

Sit down—don't disturb yourselves

(He takes off his felt hat)

MOREL and ROBIN:

Champagne from Bar-le-Duc….

MOREL:

From the depths of Lorraine!

CHAMPAGNE:

Times are hard, age comes, I intend to make a fate for myself. I'm traveling for a strong house.

ROBIN:

Which is called?

CHAMPAGNE:

You mentioned its name just now.

ROBIN:

Me?

CHAMPAGNE:

Weren't you speaking of Czar Peter the Great, sovereign of all the Russias?

ROBIN:

Indeed.

CHAMPAGNE:

Well, I'm working for him—you, for his enemies. Do the enemies of the Czar pay well?

ROBIN:

Alas, we were by way of pitying ourselves. And the Czar?

CHAMPAGNE:

I'm to receive 10,000 roubles in cash, if I bring good news to his representative The Dutchman Cornil Van Zuyp, my illustrious master.

ROBIN:

And you are in funds?

CHAMPAGNE:

There's the devil! I have good news but I do not have the first sou to return to Paris.

ROBIN:

Shake on that. We are getting some. Associate with us!

CHAMPAGNE:

Yet you are of the party of Prince Stanislas?

ROBIN: (Shrugging his shoulders)

Leave that. We will busy ourselves with him in a contrary way.

MOREL:

That will always keep us busy.

ROBIN:

What's the Czar want?

CHAMPAGNE:

The Czar has made a contract with my illustrious patron, Cornil Van Zuyp, Dutchman, man of weight, stupid like a jug, rich like a mine. By this contract, Cornil undertakes to deliver the Polish Prince to the Czar.

ROBIN:

Nice sum!

MOREL:

Equal to two million.

CHAMPAGNE:

You've already served the Czar without suspecting it, my comrades. Indeed; so long as the Prince remains in the Château de Bar, under the protection of the French government, we can do nothing against him—but if he escapes—

ROBIN:

André de Rieux is here to help him escape.

CHAMPAGNE:

May God protect Mr. André de Rieux! He's a really nice gentleman. My comrades I see a wave of roubles flooding my pockets if only we can get to Cornil Van Zuyp.

ROBIN:

It's necessary to find a nice little job.—

MOREL:

That's so.

CHAMPAGNE:

Hush! Here comes someone.

ROBIN (to BONAVENTURE):

You again!

BONAVENTURE: (Bringing a bottle and two glasses, aside)

Heavens! Now there are three of them.

MOREL:

You were told we wanted to chat.

BONAVENTURE: (Placing his bottle and glasses on a long table)

All in vain. This is a place for everybody. I'm coming to drink a round with the future master of the establishment.—who's going to marry the daughter of the owner.

FRANÇOIS: (Entering)

I am the presumptive Innkeeper of the White Horse.

CHAMPAGNE:

That's different.

(Low) We'll leave to talk.

(They talk in whispers)

BONAVENTURE: (Sitting at a table, aside)

What I want to know is does he love Madame Rosalie?

FRANÇOIS: (Aside)

I want to know how many crowns there are in the mattress of goodman Valentin.

BONAVENTURE:

To your health, neighbor.

FRANÇOIS:

Thanks. To yours.

BONAVENTURE:

All the same, you are doing a fine business.

FRANÇOIS:

Hey! Hey!

BONAVENTURE:

A heart of gold—and a fine girl. Ah, one would go far to find her like.

FRANÇOIS:

Indeed, it's true. She isn't bad looking. You that are of the house, it's true that old man Valentin, has 700 crowns hidden in his mattress?

(Aside) Now that's adroit questioning.

CHAMPAGNE: (Low)

Did you hear that?

ROBIN:

Seven hundred crowns!

MOREL:

In his mattress.

BONAVENTURE: (Aside)

He's only thinking of money.

(Aloud) And very pious and charitable. Caring for her old father, like an angel, what?

FRANÇOIS:

Ah! Hell—she's not bad! To your health!

BONAVENTURE:

To yours! A treasure.

FRANÇOIS:

In the mattress?

BONAVENTURE:

Eh, no! I am talking about Miss Rosalie.

FRANÇOIS:

I understood perfectly, but—

BONAVENTURE:

She's a treasure I am talking to you about.

FRANÇOIS:

As for me, I'm talking to you, it's necessary to have money to make a woman happy. I am not interested financially—So there are only 700 crowns in the mattress?

CHAMPAGNE: (Low)

You hear!

BONAVENTURE: (Shrugging his shoulders)

There are more than 700 crowns.

(reaction by the three adventurers)

FRANÇOIS:

There are 800?

BONAVENTURE:

Good God, man, you don't love Miss Rosalie.

FRANÇOIS:

What do you mean?

(Aside) Perhaps there are more than 800.

(Aloud) I don't love her, I who've sighed after her for so long that I am becoming skinny! 'Cause I can no longer eat or drink!—To your health!

(He drinks)

BONAVENTURE:

To yours!

FRANÇOIS:

How I dream of her, night and day, how I carved her name on the bark of poplars with my knife.

BONAVENTURE:

He actually seems to be amorous all the same. Come on, shake.

FRANÇOIS:

There are really 800—?

BONAVENTURE:

Close to it. Go put your party clothes on, my man.

(The three adventurers make signs)

You've just got time—we'll be really at ease for the party here—because we're going to receive everybody and lock the doors.

CHAMPAGNE: (Grimacing)

Sir!

ROBIN: (Low)

The devil's in it.

BONAVENTURE:

Unless some poor wretches come to demand hospitality for the love of God.

CHAMPAGNE:

For sure they will.

ROBIN:

Leave that to us.

BONAVENTURE:

Miss Rosalie is so good.

FRANÇOIS:

Send away those who pay to receive those who don't pay?

BONAVENTURE:

Huh? Is that generous?

FRANÇOIS:

For this, yes—

(Aside) It's stupid!

BONAVENTURE:

Till soon, neighbor.

FRANÇOIS:

Till soon!

(Leaving) So there are perhaps 900 crowns in the mattress.

BONAVENTURE:

Come on! This consoles me—I would have thought him more interested than this—although he thinks a bit too much of crowns. Ah, if it were me.

CHAMPAGNE:

Waiter!

BONAVENTURE: (Starting)

What?

CHAMPAGNE:

How much do we owe you?

BONAVENTURE:

A pint—twelve sous.

(The three adventurers fumble in their pockets and make a dozen sous between them.)

CHAMPAGNE: (Giving it to him)

Heavens! It's the bottom of the barrel.

(Aside) Till this evening—the crowns in the mattress.

(They leave)

ROSALIE'S VOICE: (Off)

Bonaventure! Bonaventure!

BONAVENTURE:

Ah, it's the Boss-Lady. Coming! Coming!

ROSALIE: (Entering)

There you are at last! That's lucky! I've been calling you for an hour.

(Looking at CHAMPAGNE leaving)

I don't like these vagabonds.

BONAVENTURE: (Aside, sighing)

Ah, yes—she's the most beautiful.

ROSALIE:

It's the vicinity of this prisoner that's attracting all these people. Joke of a prisoner that they allow to stroll and hunt stags in the forest. Have you seen him sometimes this prince, this Stanislas Leszczynski?

BONAVENTURE:

I don't often get out of the Inn!

ROSALIE:

That's true. They say he's quite a young man, almost a child—who often speaks of his absent mother—Dry those glasses.

BONAVENTURE:

Yes, Boss-Lady.

ROSALIE:

But there are people who want to use him to make war—Czar Peter the Great has taken his kingdom to give it to another—they've told me that story. But as for me, I recall only what concerns me—and meanwhile these new faces prowling around the neighborhood frighten me. You are going to make sure everything's locked up carefully?

BONAVENTURE:

Yes, Boss-Lady.

ROSALIE:

Don't call me that—I've told you already. My father is the one who's Boss here.—As for me, I'm only his first servant.

(She knits actively as she leaves.) Poor old father—he's sleeping.

BONAVENTURE:

But for that you wouldn't have left his bedside.

ROSALIE:

No question; it's all very simple.

BONAVENTURE:

But stay here then, a short while. Boss-Lady—that is to say, Miss Rosalie—you are working too much. That's not good sense.

ROSALIE:

I really have to work—I have folks to nourish.

BONAVENTURE:

Yes, yes, you've got them. You wouldn't take a sou from your papa for the care of old Catherine, your aunt—and the children of your late brother and of Minon your little adopted sister.

ROSALIE:

Can't you say, Miss Minon?

BONAVENTURE:

Indeed, Boss-Lady—meaning Miss Valentin—I shall say Miss Minon since you prefer that—I would really like to know what pleases you so as to do it. But I have not much wit as they say.

ROSALIE:

You don't have any at all!

BONAVENTURE: Ah, Miss Rosalie, it causes me no pain when others say it—if you knew—

ROSALIE:

Hush! Is that my father calling me?

BONAVENTURE:

No, he didn't call. All the same when I see you working like this I find it a bit much—the Boss—

ROSALIE:

He knows what money's worth.

BONAVENTURE:

One can be economical.

ROSALIE:

That's not enough when one is poor; he's miserly, he's right.

BONAVENTURE:

But you—

ROSALIE:

I am more miserly than my father.

BONAVENTURE:

Bah—! Forget it! You say that and you do good to everybody.

ROSALIE:

That's not true, it's for me, for me alone that I work, and never for the others.

BONAVENTURE:

Never? She is good—that one. Why did you take Miss Minon for your sister?

ROSALIE:

Well—it was for me, for myself alone: I wanted to please myself.

BONAVENTURE:

Ah! Bah! For you alone?

ROSALIE:

I was almost a child—I think that I was ten years old. My father was complaining of having trouble to get wherewithal to live. My father's like me—because men have often deceived him. One night I was returning from the fields I found a cradle on the sill of our door. My father who'd just opened for me, said, "Take this to the steps of the church." —There was a sleeping child in the cradle, a child of a year and a half.

BONAVENTURE:

That was Miss Minon.

ROSALIE:

The child woke up—she called her mother—when she noticed me through her tears, she smiled at me. She was a beautiful little girl wrapped in fine blankets. I said to my father, "I won't take her to the steps of the church—we'll raise her in the house." And as my father reposted about the hardness of the times and money, I said to him "The child will cost us nothing, I will nourish her."

MINON: (Who has emerged from her room and rushes into Rosalie's arms)

And you kept your word, Sis.

ROSALIE:

Ah, Minon.

MINON:

Still a child, you were already a mother.

ROSALIE:

I've indeed worked in my life—but you grew up, you called me by my name—at night my poor eyes beamed—but I heard your happy breath in your cradle. When weariness overwhelmed me too much, I sat by your bedside, only to see you. I felt as if a balm spread through my heart, and I got my courage back and I kept working. That's fine, you see, little girl, these memories.

BONAVENTURE:

And you said that you are not good, Boss-Lady!

ROSALIE:

Shut-up!

BONAVENTURE:

But Boss-Lady—

ROSALIE:

Shut-up—this time it's really him—it's my father calling me—come with me, Minon.

MINON:

Yes, Sis.

(They leave)

BONAVENTURE:

Now that's what surprises me—It's that this old man Valentin made a daughter like this. I'm going to lock up.

ANDRÉ: (Entering)

Come in, friend.

BONAVENTURE: (Aside) My, my, now another one.

(A man enters draped in his cape, hat over his eyes.)

ANDRÉ:

Wine!

(To STANISLAS) Friend, take a seat.

BONAVENTURE: (Placing wine on the table)

There!

ANDRÉ: (In a friendly way)

Leave us, my lad!

BONAVENTURE: (Leaving, aside)

At least that one is nice even when he kicks you out the door.

ANDRÉ:

Fine, we are alone.

(He rises and remains with his hat off)

I have not yet been able to pay my respects to Your Majesty.

STANISLAS: (Casting off his cloak)

You can dispense with my Majesty, Chevalier de Rieux—your hand and a truce with etiquette.

ANDRÉ:

Sire?

STANISLAS:

Do you bring me any news of my mother?

ANDRÉ:

By me, your mother the Queen sends you a thousand kisses, Sire.

STANISLAS:

My saintly mother! Speak to me of her.

ANDRÉ:

Sire, I came to speak to you about yourself. Your kingdom, oppressed by Augustus, who's only the lieutenant of Peter the Great, your kingdom awaits you and summons you.

STANISLAS: (Defeatedly)

From so far, Chevalier de Rieux, it's idle for me to lend my ear. I do not hear the voice of the fatherland.

ANDRÉ:

Sire, the voice of duty is heard everywhere.

STANISLAS: (Offended)

Sir!

ANDRÉ:

Pardon, Sire, pardon. You know whether I respect you and whether I love you. Hear me in the name of your country which was an asylum for my proscribed ancestors. King Charles the XII, The Lion of the North, the Swedish hero, the companion-in-arms, and friend of your father, King Charles XII has broken his chains.

STANISLAS:

Can it be?

ANDRÉ:

At the mere name of Charles XII, Peter the Great trembled in the depths of his icy deserts. At this name alone 20,000 gentlemen have drawn their swords beneath the walls of Cracow shouting: "Death to the Muscovites—long live Stanislas Leszczynski."

STANISLAS:

My brave gentlemen. My beloved people.

ANDRÉ:

And Charles XII, who just reached Norway, has sworn that the son of Leszczynski will re-ascend the throne of his father. He only lacks a single ally for you, Sire!

STANISLAS:

And that ally?

ANDRÉ:

It's you, yourself. You're a captive, I know—but I am coming to propose an escape for you. It's a long way to the sea from here, it's true, but our measures have been taken. From here to the ocean there are thirty post stops. Thirty devoted gentleman, disguised as postillons await you—only one post stop is not ours because the Post Master is dead: it's Nonancourt. But I'll answer for that—I'll be there at Nonancourt, André de Rieux, wearing the spurred boots and whip of a postillon.

STANISLAS:

You, Chevalier?

ANDRÉ:

I am paying my father's debt, he was hosted by Your Majesty's father.

STANISLAS:

Friend—because you are my friend…André, I thank you.

ANDRÉ:

I haven't said all, Sire. At Quilleboeuf at the mouth of the Seine a ship is awaiting you armed by the Marquis de Lauzan at his own expense. The ship is manned—by twenty-five faithful sailors. In a few days you will have crossed the Manche doubled the Danish coast, in a few days if you wish, Sire, you will find your country awakened from its sleep and very proud to see its king.

STANISLAS: (Disturbed)

My country! My beautiful fields of Warsaw—where, still a child, I saw the Sun cast splendor on the squadrons of our proud cavalry men! Oh, don't tempt me, André, don't speak further to an exile of the soil that saw his birth. Don't you see that I need all my strength to resist you? And my sanity couldn't bear it if I didn't remember my father.

ANDRÉ:

Your father?

STANISLAS:

At the hour of his death my father said to me, "Child, I pray God that you never wear the scepter or the crown."

ANDRÉ:

He was speaking as a father, because the scepter is heavy and the crown has thorns—but he wasn't speaking as King!

STANISLAS:

André, I'm resigned. Leave me in peace. Since the Czar returned to Russia, France has half opened the door of my prison. France generally treats me as a guest and not as a captive. I will be happy here, André, happier than Peter on his throne—if I could hug my dear mother.

ANDRÉ:

Your mother, the Queen, is at the Château of Saint Germain—and the Château of Saint Germain is on the road leading to the ocean.

STANISLAS:

The Queen wouldn't advise me.

ANDRÉ: (Pulling a folded letter from his breast)

I've kept this message for the final argument, Sire.

(He puts one knee on the ground and presents the letter to STANISLAS)

STANISLAS:

The Queen's handwriting—my mother's handwriting. The message contains only four words: "In passing, embrace me."

(Kissing the paper with emotion)

Chevalier, I no longer hesitate. I've never disobeyed my mother.

ANDRÉ: (Rising)

You are free at this moment. Sire, let's leave immediately.

STANISLAS:

Calm down, Chevalier. Consideration won't change my plans—my papers are at the Château—I need a few hours. Be under the ramparts at midnight.

ANDRÉ:

I'll be there with my friends, Sire.

STANISLAS:

You'll find me ready to follow you: someone's coming.

(He drapes his cape and puts on his hat)

MINON: (Coming down the stairs)

I'm going to obey my sister, I'm going to fix my dress. Ah!

(At the sight of the two men, she recoils, frightened and confused)

Pardon, gentlemen.

STANISLAS:

Don't go away, my charming child—I want to pay my bill.

ANDRÉ: (Aside)

How she blushes and how confused she is.

(Moved, smiling) I bet my heart is beating more quickly than hers.

STANISLAS:

Well—you remain on the sidelines, Chevalier?

MINON: (Aside)

He's a Chevalier—ah, I knew well enough I was crazy.

STANISLAS: (Putting a ring on his finger)

Take this, young lady—be nice more than you are pretty. (He kisses her hand) Your turn, Chevalier.

ANDRÉ: (Kissing her hand)

Remember me. (Putting a necklace around her neck) It's a blessed medallion which will bring you happiness.

(Low) I'm leaving, I love you, I shall return.

(ROSALIE goes to the doorway)

ROSALIE:

Poor papa. He dreams someone wants to take the bag which has his hoard of crowns.

ANDRÉ:

Come on, friend, to our business.

(They leave)

MINON: (Confused, aside)

Sis!

ROSALIE:

What were those men saying to you?

MINON:

They were paying their score to me.

ROSALIE:

Give me the money.

MINON: (Trembling)

It wasn't with money.

ROSALIE: (Astonished)

Ah—a necklace—a ring.

(She takes them from MINON who does not resist)

I don't know those men. But they pay their expenses richly—if they return, you will inform me.—

MINON:

Yes, yes—but (timidly points to the necklace ROSALIE has just taken) you are forgetting—

ROSALIE:

To return the necklace to you? I don't know if I ought to let you wear it. No, I'll buy you another one, but you shan't wear this one.

MINON: (Aside)

Another one! That won't be the same at all.

ROSALIE:

Meanwhile, day's over, call Bonaventure to lock everything up—and tell him not to receive anyone, François Picot and our friends will enter by the small gate in the garden. No one, you hear me, no one!

ROBIN: (Piteously)

Not even a wretch who doesn't know where to rest his head?

ROSALIE:

I recognize you. You were here just now with those men.

ROBIN:

My comrades were more lucky than I. My good lady—They found a lodging—through charity at the gate of the town—as for me, I was one too many—they sent me away.

MINON: (Who was heading toward the door, returning)

Sis, he has a nasty look.

ROSALIE:

My father said to me just now, "Never do good to men because they will do you ill for it."

ROBIN:

Oh, good lady, my gratitude.

MINON:

Sis, you are so charitable.

ROSALIE:

Mustn't be charitable—it's trickery.

MINON:

And it's so cold outside.

ROSALIE:

That's true—it is cold—rain's falling—once is not a habit. This poor man will sleep here in the low hall.

MINON: (Aside)

And I'll bring him some wedding wine.

ROSALIE: (To ROBIN)

And don't spoil anything, you will sleep without a candle.

ROBIN:

Thanks, my good lady.

ROSALIE:

Come on, kid—it's time at last for me to think of dressing up. Father won't wake up any more tonight—come help make me beautiful.

MINON:

I'm going to be your chamber-maid.

ROSALIE:

Good evening, man.

MINON:

Good evening, my friend.

ROBIN:

May God bless you. Enjoy peace—as for me, I'm going to rest.

(He heads toward the bed)

ROSALIE:

Take the lamp.

MINON:

Here it is.

(Night comes on as the two sisters leave, carrying the lamp. ROBIN rises and cocks his ear. Complete night.)

ROBIN:

The place is ours. I thought she was going to leave me outside.

(Slips toward Papa Valentin's door)

Sure they haven't put the bolt on —Open!—and the nice little lady said herself "He's sleeping." Let's be quick about it. These devilish wedding parties worry me. I prefer a house asleep. Stupid country where the betrothal takes place at midnight.

(He goes toward the window—opens it furtively and leans out)

Psst! Psst!

CHAMPAGNE: (Outside)

Psst!

ROBIN:

Climb in.

CHAMPAGNE: (Entering by the window)

It's dark as an oven.

(MOREL has the dark lantern.)

MOREL: (Entering)

I saw with the light.

ROBIN:

It will be completely night.

CHAMPAGNE:

Look! To work, who's here?

ROBIN:

An old geezer.

CHAMPAGNE:

Bah! He's sleeping—you will cut open the mattress. You'll take the hoard of money and the good man will dream his crowns are making babies.

ROBIN:

Yes, but if he wakes?

CHAMPAGNE: (Shrugging his shoulders)

That's his lookout. And you, Morel?

MOREL:

Me—we'll shoot.

CHAMPAGNE:

By the devil—shooting takes time—you are soaked chickens—keep a sharp look Out. Give me the lantern—if one has such a tender heart one becomes a nurse or a blind man's dog. Wait for me here.

(He goes into Valentin's room)

ROBIN:

He's a tough rogue, this Champagne.

MOREL:

Neither heart nor soul.

ROBIN:

He will go far. Have you seen Mr. André?

MOREL:

Everything's going fine. The Prince is going to start on the way at midnight—Mr. André gave me a big pat on the back without knowing it.

ROBIN:

Listen!

(He cocks an ear) Ah, I'll remember this night—the folks of the Inn have seen only me.

MOREL:

Bah!—It's a long way from Bar-Le-Duc to Paris.

CHAMPAGNE: (Returning pale and in disorder)

Here's the money—let's get out of here.

ROBIN:

And the old man?

CHAMPAGNE:

Put out the lantern and get going.

ROBIN:

Did the old man wake up?

CHAMPAGNE:

Here is the money, I tell you—put out the lantern and let's leave.

MOREL: (To ROBIN, low)

He woke up.

ROBIN: (Low)

May God have his soul!

(They leave by the window.—As they leave, a great tumult is heard. BONAVENTURE rushes in from Valentin's room. He's disheveled and looks around him distractedly)

ROSALIE: (Entering by the door at the right)

What's wrong? What's this noise mean?

BONAVENTURE:

The window's opened.

(Goes to look at the door of the room)

ROSALIE:

And that man is no longer here.

BONAVENTURE:

Ah, Boss-Lady, Boss-Lady.

ROSALIE:

I forbade you to call me that!

BONAVENTURE:

As long as your father was alive, Miss Rosalie.

ROSALIE:

My father!

(She rushes into the room with BONAVENTURE, ROSALIE screams then comes back on stage very pale, saying) My father, dead! Murdered!

(She falls into a chair exhausted close the door. FRANÇOIS Picot enters with the wedding guests.)

FRANÇOIS and OTHERS: Murdered!

BONAVENTURE: (Coming from the room)

Yes, those beggars—first they stole and then—

FRANÇOIS: (Aside)

Stole! Stole!

MINON: (To ROSALIE, who's opened her eyes and is looking around her, stupefied)

Sis, there's still a man who loves you.

BONAVENTURE:

Your fiancé, Boss lady.

FRANÇOIS: (Aside)

Stole! They've stolen my 800 crowns.

(A long silence. ROSALIE rises slowly.)

ROSALIE: (In an altered voice)

François, I release you from your promise.

FRANÇOIS:

I'm going to think on it. Good night everybody.

(Everyone moves away from him with disgust. He leaves.)

ROSALIE: (Falling back)

My father is dead, murdered by the man I received through charity. The one I loved abandoned me because I am poor. My father was right, men are worthless—here one must only think of oneself.

MINON: (Kneeling at her left)

Sis, My darling sister!

BONAVENTURE: (Kneeling to her right)

Ah—Boss-Lady—if you knew!

ROSALIE: (Pushing them away)

I no longer have a heart.

CURTAIN

ACT II

The hostel of the Pretty Dutch Girl.

A large and expensive main hall. Morning.

VAN ZUYP'S WIFE: (in a Prussian accent)

Countess Pfaffenhoffen, you understand. There's one I won't forget. My marriage with Mynheer Van Zuyp is a misalliance Do you comprehend? When you speak to me I intend they add to the name, wife of Van Zuyp, that I have the sorrow to bear—the title belongs to me by right of birth.—Countess Pfaffenhoffen.

COUTURIER:

Madame Countess.

WIFE:

Pfaffenhoffen!

COUTURIER:

Pfaffe.

WIFE: …hoffen—

COUTURIER: (Folding her dress)

Madame Countess Pfaffenhoffen, the more I examine your dress, the more I find—would you allow me to speak with complete frankness?

WIFE:

As you like.

COUTURIER:

Well, Madame Countess, never have I seen the Countess so miraculously dressed. There's a nobility in the cut, a grace in the draping—a harmonious ensemble.

(She admires herself)

WIFE:

A nobility—you understand—a grace—a harmony.

(To two workers) Speak without flattering.

TWO WORKERS:

It's admirable.

WIFE: (Frowning)

Well, as for me—I am very discontent, you understand?

COUTURIER:

Is it possible?

WIFE: (Harshly)

You were afraid to tell me—you understand?

(Points to her throat)

COUTURIER:

I was not.

WIFE:

You were wrong! I told you a very plain dress.

COUTURIER:

There's not one ribbon.

WIFE: That's the rub—it doesn't resemble the dress of Countess Pfaffenhoffen....

COUTURIER:

If Madame Countess would like....

(She gestures to her assistant, who opens a box)

WIFE:

I seem too much like a wife of Van Zuyp—Although Mynheer Van Zuyp will not remain always a bourgeois—He's going to buy a Marquis' title this year, you understand?

COUTURIER: (Placing the box in front of the Countess)

If Madame would be so good as to choose some ribbons?

WIFE: (Making her choice)

This is not to please the other sex, you know? Ah, I don't concern myself with the other sex. I'm taking these ribbons only to put on my shoulder.

COUTURIER:

That will be in perfect taste.

(She attaches them)

WIFE:

I'm taking these roses only to cover my throat.

COUTURIER: (Attaching them)

These two colors match marvelously.

WIFE:

These two materials below—this to the belt.

COUTURIER: (With admiration)

Ah, Madame Countess—what delicate taste.

WIFE:

Fix it so it's still very simple.

COUTURIER: (Attaching bows in the back)

That's easy, Madame Countess.

WIFE:

I love that which is simple—How do you like it?

COUTURIER:

Words fail me. These young girls are mute, too.

WIFE: (Returning the box)

There aren't many ribbons, you know in your box.

(ANDRÉ half opens the door at the left)

O heaven! A person of the opposite sex. Don't leave me.

COUTURIER:

We shall remain close to Madame Countess.

ANDRÉ: (Entering)

Madame Countess….

(He stops as if stuck by admiration)

WIFE: (To COUTURIER)

Don't leave me. If this gentleman were to lack respect for me—

ANDRÉ:

Ah! Madame! Blessed be the fate which allowed me to get to you. I was seeking you.

WIFE: (To COUTURIER)

He was looking for me—you know, get out!

COUTURIER:

Madame Countess doesn't fear?

WIFE:

Since he was seeking me, you understand.

COUTURIER:

That's true. Let's go, young ladies.

WIFE:

Next time, put more ribbons in your box.

COUTURIER: (In the door way)

Ah! What a dress! What a dress!

(All three leave, making deep curtsies and signs of admiration)

(ANDRÉ is dressed in very elegant town clothes)

WIFE: (Modestly showing her dress)

It was very bold to receive you in negligée—but traveling—in a hostel, and then if she'd had more ribbons in her box.

ANDRÉ:

What you have suffices, Madame.

WIFE:

Do you think so, I allow you to kiss the ends of my fingers—with respect.

ANDRÉ:

A thousand graces!

(Kissing her hand, aside) She's mad as hatter. But this is the only way I can obtain this commission.

WIFE: (Sighing)

Ah! Chevalier! Chevalier! You've compromised me in the eyes of my dress-maker.

ANDRÉ:

Compromised!

WIFE:

Black hair. That's precisely the color I prefer.

ANDRÉ:

Madame, yesterday, at the court ball you gave me permission to come ask you a favor.

WIFE:

Mynheer Cornil Van Zuyp is very jealous, you know?

ANDRÉ:

Don't worry, Madame, it's a question of a good deed.

WIFE: (Disappointed)

Ah—we pass for very charitable in the Pfaffenhoffen country.

ANDRÉ:

I know that by your position and the immense fortune of Mr. Van Zuyp you have complete power in the Superintendent's office. I'd like to have for a very wretched woman the office of Post of the Nonancourt office—which is presently vacant.

WIFE:

Do you know, Chevalier—I never do anything for women.

ANDRÉ:

Pity, beautiful lady.

WIFE:

I thought you were asking something for yourself, Chevalier?

ANDRÉ:

As for me, I have many things to tell you, Madame Countess.

(Aside) Ah! The devil! I was forgetting my role.

(Aloud) If you allow me, I will come myself this evening to seek the commission.

WIFE:

You know—I'll permit it—on condition you have some respect.

ANDRÉ:

And you promise.

WIFE:

I promise.

ANDRÉ:

Ah! How many favors, beautiful lady.

(At the moment he takes leave by kissing her hand, a sewing girl enters pressured by CORNIL who tries to grab her by the waist. CORNIL and his wife find themselves face to face. ANDRÉ bows and leaves.)

WIFE:

My husband!

CORNIL: (Aside)

My wife.

(To sewing girl) Leave!

WIFE:

And bring me my chocolate, do you know—? Bold face!

CORNIL:

Wife Van Zuyp, you are as beribboned as the shrine of Abraham at Maestricht. I pay you a compliment on that handsome young man.

WIFE:

The virtue of Countess Pfaffenhoffen is above your insinuations, Mynheer Cornil.

CORNIL:

I find nothing to reply to that. One must howl with wolves. For my business we need to please the Regent, and the Regent doesn't like strict morals—As for myself, I try to take on allures.

WIFE:

Fie, will you! As for me, if I wanted I could easily assume this frivolity—this do—whatever you like—Mr. Champagne told me it was the French way. New there's a well brought up man, this Mr. de Champagne—But you, you will always be a bourgeois—Mynheer Cornil.

CORNIL:

It's a question of earning a million rubles by delivering Prince Stanislas to the Czar. Mr. de Champagne is going to make some friends for me—I've already supped with great lords.

WIFE:

What did they say to you?

CORNIL:

They asked me if I would loan them money.

WIFE:

It must have been very nice, a little supper?

CORNIL:

It's very slatternly.

WIFE: (Aside)

I'd really like to see a little supper. But here's that dear Mr. Champagne.

CHAMPAGNE: (Enters in a costume of a very well turned out gentleman)

Health to the glory of Holland! Beautiful lady, I bend my respect at your feet.

(He bows with a breezy way, placing his hat under his arm and turning on his heel)

WIFE:

Mr. de Champagne—you know—I'd like to see a little supper—you understand.

CHAMPAGNE:

Perfectly.

CORNIL: (To CHAMPAGNE)

Let's talk business.

(Turning to his wife) Wife Van Zuyp.

WIFE:

Born Countess Pfaffenhoffen,

CORNIL:

I have grave political interests to discuss with Mr. de Champagne.

WIFE:

I'll retire.

(Low to CHAMPAGNE) You found him for me?

CHAMPAGNE:

What?

WIFE:

The little dancing master.

CHAMPAGNE:

Yes.

WIFE:

What color?

CHAMPAGNE:

Blond going on red.

WIFE:

Oh—the color I love the best. Do you know?—Mr. Champagne. We'll allow you to kiss our hand.

(She leaves after deep curtsies)

CORNIL:

Where were we—?

CHAMPAGNE:

Prince Stanislas.

CORNIL:

The other business, Mr. Champagne, the other business—The wife of Van Zuyp cannot hear us any longer. The love affair—The great affair!

CHAMPAGNE: (Aside)

He's taken the bait

(Aloud) It's not the most pressing thing, boss.

CORNIL:

Indeed! I perfectly grasped your ideas. You told me that it was necessary for me to have a mistress to be at the top. At the court of the Regent, a man without a mistress is unlucky. As I have plenty of money, I require a mistress without peer, a pearl, a diamond. You've taken it on yourself to find me that.

(shaking) Huh!

(laughing) I thought it was the spouse of Van Zuyp.

CHAMPAGNE:

Thing promised, thing done.

CORNIL:

Then you've found—

CHAMPAGNE:

I found the pearl, I found the diamond—in my travels

CORNIL:

Where was that?

CHAMPAGNE:

In Bar-Le-Duc—a young girl.

CORNIL:

Pretty?

CHAMPAGNE:

Adorable!

CORNIL:

And who will be spoken of?

CHAMPAGNE:

From her debut—

CORNIL:

And of me?

CHAMPAGNE:

By reflection.

CORNIL:

But why go seek her at such a distance?

CHAMPAGNE:

I have my reasons. You are going to see, let's leave the love affair for a moment—

CORNIL:

Already?

CHAMPAGNE:

And let's return to the young Prince. He escaped three days ago from the Château of Bar-Le-Duc—where the French government was holding him prisoner. The thing is known in Paris and the Minister has given orders to his agents to arrest His Highness.

CORNIL:

Good.

CHAMPAGNE:

Bad! If the Regent's government seeks to take him back it's to protect him against us, against the attempt of the Czar, for his safety and not to deliver him to his enemies.

CORNIL:

In that case, what to do?

CHAMPAGNE:

Steal a march on the French police, I have some devoted men of whom I am immediately going to show you a specimen. Seeing the time that has elapsed since his escape, Stanislas must necessarily be wandering about the environs of Paris. His mother resides in the Château of Saint—Germain-en-Laye. I've set up ambushes in the forest, if he attempts to approach his mother, we've got him.

CORNIL:

Very good—Mr. de Champagne, I am pleased with you.

CHAMPAGNE:

I haven't finished, if he avoids my trap at Saint Germain, we will catch him at Nonancourt. That post is vacant—we need to have a woman who belongs to us, completely to us.

CORNIL:

Have you also found this woman?

CHAMPAGNE:

Yes.

CORNIL:

In your travels?

CHAMPAGNE:

At Bar-Le-Duc

CORNIL:

Again! So you find everything at Bar-Le-Duc

CHAMPAGNE:

A determined woman, avaricious, selfish. She's boasts about herself this way at every opportunity. A woman who no longer has anything in the world.

(Aside) Thanks to me.

(Aloud) And who is in the position to sell her soul to the highest bidder.

CORNIL:

In a word, a treasure.

CHAMPAGNE:

A treasure. I've written this woman to come to Paris immediately to the hostel, the Beautiful Dutch girl, where we are, and I've promised her the post of Nonancourt. Have I too much prejudiced your credit?

CORNIL:

I'll have the commission this evening.

CHAMPAGNE:

The nice part of this story is that the treasure and the pearl are sisters.

CORNIL:

Truly!

CHAMPAGNE:

With this commission we kill two birds with one shot. We have Rosalie, the elder sister, who will deliver the Prince to us, and Minon, the younger sister, whose ingenuous beauty will lend you the gallant relief that you lack.

CORNIL:

It's perfect.

CHAMPAGNE:

But—I promised you to show you a specimen of my men (rings).

CORNIL:

They are scoundrels, your men.

CHAMPAGNE:

Determined ones.

CORNIL:

So much the better, that's needed for this business.

CHAMPAGNE: (To a servant)

Show in those two brave men who are waiting in the vestibule.

CORNIL:

Yes, show them in! Ah, ah, if they'd told me in Holland that I would have relations one day with malefactors (with pride) I have indeed got on the right road—I've got the conscience needed for it.

(MOREL and ROBIN enter)

CHAMPAGNE:

Boss I present to you friend Robin and friend Morel, your devoted servants.

ROBIN:

For devotion, you see.

MOREL:

Ah! As for that—

CORNIL: (Looking at them through his lorgnette)

They are ugly—They are very ugly—

CHAMPAGNE:

For what they have to do—

CORNIL:

That's true—

CHAMPAGNE:

Boss, give them some kind words so they'll encourage their comrades….

CORNIL:

Gladly—Hah!, Hah!, Hah! My friends, I've come to Paris to earn money—I am rich. I have twenty-eight vessels on the seas of India. I have counters, I have fishermen, I have factories,—but I want to earn more money. Much more money, to earn money spend a little. I'll spend a little on you—Here….

(He tosses them his purse)

Be economical and serve me well.

(To CHAMPAGNE) How's that?

CHAMPAGNE:

It's more than eloquent; it's stupendous.

CORNIL:

I was cut out to speak in public. I am going to work for the commission. Till soon.

(He leaves)

CHAMPAGNE, ROBIN, MOREL: (Bowing to CORNIL as he leaves)

Good evening, Milord.

CHAMPAGNE: (Lowering his voice)

What news?

ROBIN:

The one we are pursuing is in Paris.

CHAMPAGNE:

You're sure of it?

ROBIN:

I've seen him.

MOREL:

Me, too.

CHAMPAGNE:

Alone?

ROBIN:

Not at all—with Mr. André, our former patron.

MOREL:

Five gentlemen of his country and a dozen musketeers of the king met yesterday evening at Porcherons—under the presidency of the Marquis de Lauzun. André de Rieux and Prince Stanislas were there.

ROBIN:

They drank champagne—they shouted, "Long live Charles XII!"

CHAMPAGNE:

And the Prince's itinerary?

ROBIN:

Still the same, Saint Germain, Nonancourt, etc.

CHAMPAGNE:

That's fine.

ROBIN:

There's something that isn't so fine—

CHAMPAGNE:

What's that?

ROBIN:

The woman from Bar-Le-Duc, the hostess of the Inn.

MOREL:

Miss Rosalie Valentin.

CHAMPAGNE: (Excitedly)

Is she in Paris, too?

ROBIN:

Exactly.

CHAMPAGNE:

Bravo!

ROBIN:

What do you mean, bravo! If she recognizes me—

CHAMPAGNE:

She's only seen you once. You will avoid her. For us she's worth her weight in gold. Robin, I direct you to watch over the Prince. Morel, you will get the woman from Bar-Le-Duc to come to this hostel. So my pretties, you will make a fortune, and I'm the one who's telling you so,—with this fat Dutchman. Keep on the trail carefully. I'll take care of the rest.

ROBIN:

When will it be necessary to rejoin our men in the forest of Saint-Germain?

CHAMPAGNE:

I will see you this evening in the cabaret of Saint-Merry.

ROBIN:

In that case, till tonight.

MOREL:

Till tonight.

(They leave)

CHAMPAGNE:

It seems there's man under the thick skin of this Dutch merchant—This Mynheer Cornil is enflamed before even having seen the little one. Sonofabitch! From the two millions, Mynheer Cornil will give me 100,000 pounds. I prefer to do the thing on my own account and not give him anything at all.

SERVANT: (Entering)

The Countess wishes to speak to you, Mr. de Champagne.

CHAMPAGNE:

I'll be right there.

(Servant leaves)

CHAMPAGNE:

Van Zuyp's wife is too friendly toward me.

SERVANT: (Re-entering)

The Countess is very urgent.

CHAMPAGNE:

Coming, coming.

(He leaves)

(ANDRÉ appears in the rear and looks attentively at CHAMPAGNE)

ANDRÉ: (Watching CHAMPAGNE leave)

I'm not mistaken, that man is actually the one my friends pointed out to me—he's the damned soul of Milord Van Zuyp. The two of them are battling me without knowing me, I hope. Both have sworn to ruin the Prince. As for me, I'll save him despite himself if need be. He's imprudent! What's he doing at this moment? He forgets, at Saint-Germain, near his mother, the danger which threatens him, his head has a Russian price on it, the steel of assassins ready to strike him in the shadows. Oh—I will go join him, lead him away, demand that he leave once I am assured of this commission I am waiting for, that this ridiculous Countess promised me news of at the Nonancourt post.

BONAVENTURE'S VOICE: (Under the window)

Don't be afraid, I have a strong back, Boss-Lady.

ANDRÉ:

The Boss-Lady—I know that voice.

(Looks at the window) Bonaventure—and near him our pretty Innkeeper of Bar-Le-Duc and her sister Minon—always charming. But

I do not yet have that Brevet and then they mustn't see me dressed like this. Save yourself if you can.

(He leaves by the right)

ROSALIE: (Entering)

I cannot go on.

(MINON seems overwhelmed with packages, suitcases; she holds an umbrella in her hand, ROSALIE looks around her)

It's nice here, it must be very expensive.

MINON:

Ah, how worn out I am.

BONAVENTURE:

This Parisian pavement wears out the soles of your feet. Can I put down the effects, Boss-Lady?

ROSALIE:

Not yet.

(BONAVENTURE remains loaded down)

They told me to come here and that I would find protectors here—because I received two letters—both promising me the Post Bureau at Nonancourt.

BONAVENTURE:

Two letters by the same hand.

ROSALIE:

No, two different handwritings.

BONAVENTURE:

And you knew them? That's odd, indeed! Ah, yes, Boss-Lady.

MINON: (Aside)

I seemed to see him at the window. I think I see him everywhere! I'm going mad!

ROSALIE:

Finally, I decided to leave, and my word! I sold everything down there—The house and the furniture. It was making me ill, what to see the door of father's room. And the window through which the murderer passed. My poor father—Ah, it was I, who killed him by giving asylum to that wretched beggar. His murderer, no question, and since then impossible to catch that man, impossible. Still, I can no longer live in that unlucky house. I made a bundle of my clothes and here I am. As for me, I'm never embarrassed.

BONAVENTURE:

As for that, no, Boss-Lady.

ROSALIE:

There's one who would be embarrassed with my errands—for I bring my errands here—with me.

BONAVENTURE:

Me, too, I have my errands—

ROSALIE:

Old Aunt Catherine.

BONAVENTURE:

And the little one—always kind, the Boss-Lady.

ROSALIE:

Ah, indeed—there's no one here? I want to ask for a room—inexpensive—

MINON:

Here's someone.

BONAVENTURE:

It's fine company, Boss-Lady.

CHAMPAGNE: (To CORNIL)

Here's the young person.

CORNIL:

She's beautiful.

(He lorgnettes MINON)

Very beautiful.

ROSALIE: (To BONAVENTURE, pointing to CHAMPAGNE)

Haven't I seen this lord somewhere?

BONAVENTURE:

At our place, at Bar-Le-Duc.

WIFE: (To CHAMPAGNE)

Do you know—that young man there—I really like the color of his hair.

CHAMPAGNE: (To ROSALIE)

Come, Madame Valentin—for you must be called Madame, down there, at the Post.

ROSALIE: (Astonished)

At the Post?

CHAMPAGNE:

We are old acquaintances, Madame Valentin. I am going to deliver your commission to you.

ROSALIE:

Then it was you who wrote me?

CHAMPAGNE:

Myself.

ROSALIE: (Suspicious)

And why are you interesting yourself in me?

CHAMPAGNE:

Come, you shall know.

(Makes a sign to CORNIL)

ROSALIE:

So, be it, come, Minon.

CORNIL: (Leaving last)

What a figure! In Holland the women don't resemble this.

WIFE: (To BONAVENTURE who wants to leave as well)

Stay, you know;

(All leave except wife and BONAVENTURE)

BONAVENTURE:

Leave me alone, will you. I want to go with the Boss-Lady.

WIFE:

(Holding him by the umbrella that he holds in his hand,) You understand—I have to speak to you, I noticed you.

BONAVENTURE:

So what, let me go.

WIFE: (Aside)

This lad is very innocent.

(Aloud) Will you be my footman?

BONAVENTURE:

What's that?

WIFE:

That's a handsome lad who mounts behind the carriage.

BONAVENTURE:

I intend to go with the Boss-Lady.

WIFE:

The Boss-Lady, The Boss-Lady—look at my dress?

BONAVENTURE:

Oh—the funny looking dress all the same. She's from Auvergne.

WIFE:

Will you be my footman?

BONAVENTURE:

Is she funny this Savoyard?

WIFE:

Countess Pfaffenhoffen—from Prussia.

BONAVENTURE:

Make way—Countess Fauferlucken! Ah, why I'm running after the Boss-Lady—Let me alone, will you, Andalousian.

(He leaves his umbrella in the hands of the Countess and rushes after ROSALIE)

WIFE:

He left me his umbrella in my hand.

(Pulling a letter from her breast)

But I have wherewith to console myself. The brown young man has written me. Let's see what he says. He requests me to deliver the commission to Rosalie Valentin who is in this Inn. I understand she is here—Here she is—I'm going to utter, some dignified words to her in delivering this commission to her.

ROSALIE: (Enters holding a parchment)

I've got it, this commission—here it is. I don't know why they are casting it at my head, but who cares?—Mistress of Post at Nonancourt!

MINON:

Sis!

BONAVENTURE:

Boss-Lady.

ROSALIE:

That's fine—I know you—Oh, I know you—some luck comes to me, you are going to caress me—by Jove.

BONAVENTURE:

Ah, what are you talking about?

ROSALIE:

You're worth more than the rest of them, aren't you?

(With irony) So be calm, I believe in your affection.

(Laughs) Yes, yes.

(Wife approaches her and touches her lightly on the shoulder) Huh! What do you want with me? Who is this lady here?

WIFE: (To ROSALIE)

Madame?

ROSALIE:

Madame!

WIFE:

It's pleasant to spread and practice good deeds around oneself—like the Sun—star of day, you understand which warms up the vegetables and the insects, you understand? Here's the commission which will save you from misfortune.

ROSALIE:

The commission? It's the second.

BONAVENTURE:

It's raining them.

WIFE:

No thanks, my reward is in my heart.

(Aside) I wish the brown young man were able to hear me.

ROSALIE: (Astonished)

Thanks, Madame.

WIFE: (Moving away, proudly)

I withdraw from your gratitude.

BONAVENTURE: (Stopping her)

Give me back my umbrella, Scotswoman.

(She gives him the umbrella and leaves)

ROSALIE: Two commissions—why two commissions?

BONAVENTURE:

It's funny, all the same. Boss-Lady, I've got my umbrella back.

ROSALIE:

Bah—this proves I have more than one protector.

BONAVENTURE:

That's certain. (Caressing his umbrella) I was afraid of not seeing it again.

(ANDRÉ appears at the door dressed as a postillon)

MINON: (Seeing him)

Ah!

ROSALIE:

What's wrong with you?

MINON:

Nothing, Sis.

BONAVENTURE: (Noticing ANDRÉ)

Oh, the poacher who's become a postillon.

MINON: (Aside)

Just now, in the window, he was dressed as a gentleman.

ANDRÉ: (Advancing confidently)

Greetings, Boss-Lady—this lad speaks the truth—from poacher I become postillon—and if you like, I will be yours at the post of Nonancourt.

ROSALIE:

Truly.

(To BONAVENTURE and MINON) What do the rest of you think about it?

BONAVENTURE:

As for me, I say I wouldn't take him.

(Aside) He's too handsome.

ROSALIE:

And you, Minon?

(ANDRÉ makes supplicating signs to MINON)

MINON: (After a struggle)

I am of the same opinion as Bonaventure.

ROSALIE:

Goodness, goodness.

(She goes to ANDRÉ and examines him)

Fine, everyone is of the opinion not to engage this lad—as for me, I will take him.

ANDRÉ:

Fine! Thanks, Boss-Lady.

MINON: (Aside)

I did what I could; this isn't my fault.

ROSALIE: (To ANDRÉ)

Come on, let's leave for Nonancourt! You're the one who will lead us there—

ANDRÉ:

Yes, Boss-Lady.

ROSALIE:

We must go there straightaway.

ANDRÉ:

We will go directly there. All on the way! On the way!

CHAMPAGNE: (Appearing at the rear, the Chevalier de Rieux as postillon)

As for me, without changing outfit I'll take his master, and his mistress from him!

(Preparations for departure)

CURTAIN

ACT III

ANDRÉ and STANISLAS enter from the office, furtively just as CORNIL and CHAMPAGNE leave. ANDRÉ is dressed as a gentleman, with a cloak.

ANDRÉ:

Finally they've gone. Ah! Prince, you've gambled madly with your life and the future of your crown.

STANISLAS: (Also as a gentleman)

I cannot separate myself from my mother.

ANDRÉ:

Everything was ready, down there, at Nonancourt. I was expecting you from moment to moment. A day passed, then two days—I was unable to control my impatience—I rushed and I found the forest full of traps and guarded. paths—You yourself worn out and almost discouraged by your fruitless efforts.

STANISLAS:

No, not discouraged, friend—a little rest is all I need—All the same, I've had a lot of happiness in my misfortune—when they drove me back to the edge of the woods, I observed at the park entrance my mother's carriage and we were able to exchange a last kiss from a distance.

ANDRÉ:

I won't leave you, Sire.—I promised the Queen and I am a gentleman.

STANISLAS:

My poor mother! I'll never see her again! And who knows if I ever return to my kingdom?

ANDRÉ:

What are you saying?

STANISLAS:

These traps, these treacheries, by which I am surrounded. You know friend, that I don't fear death, death on my country's soil surrounded, by my faithful soldiers, like a cavalier, like a king. Ah, that glorious death, if it is reserved for me, blessed be the will of God. But to fall, an obscure sacrifice, without having had time to unsheathe a sword, to fall struck down by an assassin, and on the soil of France ah, that idea is horrible and makes me lose all my courage.

ANDRÉ:

Sire, my friends and I, will keep a good guard around you, we will out smart agents in the employ of the foreigner. For France has never been the accomplice of such treacheries. France, even under the control of a Dubois, keeps its great natural heart. The generous heart of the most generous nation in the world. All the same, there's only one serious danger for you—just one—the passage through the forest of Saint Germain—I am sure of the Post of Nonancourt. It's mainly a question of extending and repairing the three days you have wasted.

STANISLAS:

Wasted? I spent them near my mother.

ANDRÉ:

Those three days have doubled the difficulty of our undertaking, we can no longer think of finding horses. I am going to leave to prepare things down there—you'll rest on route, at the first inn—and you will rejoin me.

STANISLAS:

I'm putting myself in your hand, Chevalier—let's part.

ANDRÉ:

Let's part! Madame Valentin—Ah!

(They leave as ROSALIE enters)

ROSALIE: (Enters in rage, her hands full of utensils)

Look, the rest of you—people are neither slow nor clever in this country. Where are the employees of this inn? The fakers!

(With increasing rage) One Queen! One Queen of Poland! That's not a reason to spatter an respectable woman.

BONAVENTURE:

As for that Boss-Lady, she didn't badly splash you but you didn't want to straighten yourself out.

ROSALIE:

Straighten myself out—and why? The highway is no longer for everyone now

BONAVENTURE:

I'm going to tell you—a carriage—it's a carriage.

ROSALIE:

As for me, I splash no one.

BONAVENTURE:

Calm down—it's not her fault.

ROSALIE: (To Porters)

Come on, look, let's bestir ourselves, these sacks of hay to be covered—you will pay me for them if it rains?

BONAVENTURE:

Come on, look sharp—let's bestir ourselves. Come on, look sharp.

(To ROSALIE) It's going to be done, Boss-Lady, it's going to be done.

ROSALIE:

By Jove, it better be or we will see!

(The porters arrange the sacks and the employees of the inn help)

BONAVENTURE:

Sit down, Boss-Lady.

ROSALIE: (Drying her face)

(To a serving girl) Look, mother of God!—My life! Is it you or me they pay here to be a serving girl of the inn? Rid me of all this and be quick about it!

BONAVENTURE:

Look, look sharp—some energy, girl!

SERVING GIRL:

I'm doing all I can.

ROSALIE:

No back talk. I don't like that.

BONAVENTURE: (To the serving girl)

The Boss-Lady doesn't like it, what! Each to his taste.

ROSALIE: (Calming down a little)

Thank God I made purchases. My purse is flat, and so many things remain for me to buy. Ah, it's rough. A post for horses.

(To porter) You're going to break that pottery, bandylegs. Do you have the money to replace it for me? Where are our postillons—the lazy bones! Dancing, I wager.

(To the serving girl who come closer) What! Are you lurking there to listen to us, slut? You won't make old bones around me, I warn you. Here, take this to my basket.

(She gives her packages) Needles, here are no better than those at Nonancourt, but they cost more. Spiced bread for the children—they sell the same at the home of the grocer opposite us. Tobacco for Aunt Catherine. Ah, this is a surprise for Minon.

BONAVENTURE:

For Miss Minon?

(The serving girl moves away)

ROSALIE: (To BONAVENTURE)

Can you see her from here, showing me her beautiful white teeth when smiling with all her heart?

BONAVENTURE:

That's still amusing! It seems to me that I do see her.

ROSALIE:

Do you hear her saying to me with her sweet little voice, "Thanks, dear Sis."

BONAVENTURE:

I do hear her, Boss-Lady.

ROSALIE:

Ah, it's not money wasted.

BONAVENTURE:

No saying that. She becomes sweeter every day.

ROSALIE: (Looking at him, astonished)

You think so?

BONAVENTURE:

At a glance, Boss-Lady, at a glance….

ROSALIE:

Ah, you noticed it, did you?

BONAVENTURE: (Modestly)

Ah, yes—all the same though, without seeming to….

ROSALIE:

Sweetness—it's useless—and that ends only too quickly.

(Pulling other object from her pocket)

Seeds for the garden.

BONAVENTURE:

Flowers that you loved in Lorraine, Boss-Lady—flowers grow everywhere.

ROSALIE:

You don't need to fear being betrayed by such friends.

BONAVENTURE: (Aside)

Now there she goes thinking of François Picot. Ah, if only I could console her.

ROSALIE:

A puppet, a reed pipe, a drum so as to wake my ears.

BONAVENTURE:

At least, you are nice enough, Boss-Lady.

ROSALIE:

I advise you to beware of it! Don't you see, I'm doing this all for me? So, at bottom, I care nothing for others.

BONAVENTURE:

What! It's for you? The puppet, the reed pipe, and the drum, too?

ROSALIE: (Shrugging her shoulders)

It's so as to see them twist around me, when I return. Minon, sly and quite red with curiosity—Aunt Catherine shaking her head and opening her large greedy eyes—the restless children, urgent gourmands, like little wolves, hugging your knees, sniffing your pockets to guess from the odor what you bring—It's the world in miniature, my poor Bonaventure, you see. Children, young folks, old geezers give you a party only on the condition of having their gifts.

BONAVENTURE: (Laughing)

Hell! Listen, will you, Boss-Lady, little gifts—hey, hey, hey!

ROSALIE: (Roughly)

Don't laugh like that.

BONAVENTURE: (Cutting off his laughing)

See, I'm not laughing.

ROSALIE:

You are right not to laugh. See, it's sad, it's desolating. That's why I'm suspicious of the whole world—that's why I love no one!

BONAVENTURE:

Ah!—No one.

ROSALIE:

No one—Let's see—What have I still to buy?

BONAVENTURE:

Two change horses for the Regent's relays.

ROSALIE:

I've got my opportunity. A Parisian with lands in Normandy—who told me he'd come find me here. It's an opportunity.

BONAVENTURE:

Hay for the season.

ROSALIE:

The Parisian has hay.

BONAVENTURE:

Bran, straw....

ROSALIE:

The Parisian has bran and straw. Money! Do I have enough money to buy all this? Happily these Parisians are easy to trick.

(To the serving girl who returns) You again?

SERVING GIRL:

I came to see if you have need of me.

BONAVENTURE:

Need of me—What talk!

ROSALIE:

Go see down there if I am here, girl!

SERVING GIRL:

I really want to....

(She starts to leave)

BONAVENTURE:

What a mouth!

ROSALIE: (To serving girl)

Hold on—someone's going to ask for me—a gentleman—send him to me.

SERVING GIRL:

That's what!

BONAVENTURE:

Why, what a mouth, Boss-Lady.

(The serving girl leaves, the porters have left. All action ceases on stage)

ROSALIE:

You are going to see how I'm going to swindle the Parisian.

BONAVENTURE:

Yes, we're going to see that, Boss-Lady.

ROSALIE:

Now, we are alone, Bonaventure, let's chat. Sit down near me—close. I have an idea and I want to ask your advice.

BONAVENTURE: (Astonished)

My advice?

ROSALIE:

Don't sit on the edge of your chair—squat on it like a man! There! Do you think you're worth less than those who are more proud than you are?

BONAVENTURE: (Trembling)

Ah, Boss-Lady—Thanks, really, all the same.

ROSALIE:

I want to ask your advice because you have good sense and good faith. It's nice these days—listen to me carefully—look, my boy, I will live to be very old, I'm sure of it.

BONAVENTURE:

May it please God, Boss-Lady.

ROSALIE:

God will ordain it. In my home as they say, the sword blade doesn't wear out the scabbard. I don't ruin my blood. I eat well. I sleep well—Why? Because I think only of myself from morn to midnight.

BONAVENTURE: (Smiling)

Will you do that?

ROSALIE:

I really pity those who beat their brains out thinking of others. They must be naïve.

BONAVENTURE:

They've got to be stupid and even goofy.

ROSALIE:

My poor father said it right. Everyone for himself.

BONAVENTURE:

After me, the end of the world.

ROSALIE:

So it's understood I'll live to be real old.

BONAVENTURE:

It's understood, Boss-Lady.

ROSALIE:

Consequently, when I get married….

BONAVENTURE: (Shaking)

Huh?—Oh! Are you thinking of remarrying, Boss-Lady?

ROSALIE:

What do you mean, remarrying? You do not imagine I am the widow of François Picot, who is not dead and who I didn't marry! Don't interrupt me, gossiper!

BONAVENTURE: (Sadly)

No, Boss-Lady.

ROSALIE:

When I go get married, I intend to take a very young man—because I said to myself (always the egoist you see, that's my character; no need to rehash that)—because I said to myself—If you take a man older than you, when you get to be sixty, you will have an old geezer around you that must be cared for.

BONAVENTURE:

That's quite certain! Now that's thinking!

ROSALIE:

While, on the contrary, I'm the one who wants to be cared for—coddled, spoiled

BONAVENTURE:

And you are dammed right!

ROSALIE:

It's a good idea, or not?

BONAVENTURE:

Ah, yes, Boss-Lady—as for that, it's a sparkling idea.

ROSALIE: (Confidently)

See then, Bonaventure.

BONAVENTURE:

What about, Boss-Lady?

ROSALIE:

Have you noticed that handsome postillon?

BONAVENTURE:

The former poacher—Mr. André?

ROSALIE:

A nice name, I think, Mr. André.

BONAVENTURE:

That depends on taste—Miss Minon also finds that name nice—as for myself….

ROSALIE: (Looking at him)

Eh! There you are all sad? What's wrong with you that makes you sigh, my poor Bonaventure?

BONAVENTURE:

Me?

ROSALIE:

God forgive me, you have tears in your eyes?

BONAVENTURE: (Drying his eyes)

Ah, Boss-Lady, if you knew.

ROSALIE: (Smiling)

By Jove! It's not difficult to guess, my lad. I wasn't born yesterday; just now you said, that Minon's a pretty sprig of girl.

BONAVENTURE:

I said that?

ROSALIE:

Now you say with an annoyed manner, that Minon finds the name André to her taste. You love her, my friend. It's clear as day—.

BONAVENTURE: (Reproachfully)

Ah, Boss-Lady, now that's not nice.

ROSALIE:

What harm is there in that?

BONAVENTURE:

If you knew, Boss-Lady.

ROSALIE: (Looking at him, aside)

This young lad is so nice. He'll make Minon so happy.

BONAVENTURE:

Miss Minon.

ROSALIE:

Getting back to handsome André.

BONAVENTURE:

Hold it, Boss-Lady, would you like my frank opinion?

ROSALIE:

No question!

BONAVENTURE:

Well—

(Hesitating) If you knew—

ROSALIE:

Yes, I know.

CHAMPAGNE: (In the Inn)

I am asking for Madame Valentin.

ROSALIE:

It's the Parisian. We'll talk of this again.

BONAVENTURE: (Aside)

I'll never dare to say that to her—If you knew….

CHAMPAGNE: (Entering)

There she is, there she is, that dear Madame Valentin.

BONAVENTURE: (Aside)

That face again.

CHAMPAGNE:

Well, are we going to do business together?

ROSALIE:

Why, it's you, Sir, the proprietor of those lands in Normandy?

BONAVENTURE: (To ROSALIE)

He hadn't six sous in the times of Bar-Le-Duc.

CHAMPAGNE:

Eh, yes, it's me—Do you know, dear lady, that we are now, old acquaintances?

ROSALIE:

Indeed!

CHAMPAGNE:

I drank in your inn in Lorraine—and, be it said in passing, you are going to understand soon why I was wandering about there.

ROSALIE:

I am not curious.

CHAMPAGNE:

Some days later, in Paris, I obtained the Post of Nonancourt, a good position—

ROSALIE:

And you promised to inform me?

CHAMPAGNE:

Why, if I served you in such an obliging way—dear lady, it was in view of an affair we are going to conclude today.

ROSALIE:

To sell me horses, hay, and straw?

CHAMPAGNE:

It's really a question of straw, hay, and horses?

(To BONAVENTURE) Friend, they are having fun down there without you—don't you want to have a turn dancing?

ROSALIE:

So, this is a secret?

BONAVENTURE: (To ROSALIE)

Be careful!

CHAMPAGNE:

A big secret!

ROSALIE: (To BONAVENTURE)

Go, my friend.

BONAVENTURE:

Yes, Boss-Lady.

(Aside, leaving) I'm going to keep an eye on this here landowner.

(He leaves)

CHAMPAGNE: (Leaning closer)

It's a political matter.

ROSALIE: (Astonished)

Political?

CHAMPAGNE:

Politics is what makes you fat.

ROSALIE:

I warn you that politics and I, we don't go together.

CHAMPAGNE:

If you permit me, I am going to give you a lesson—

ROSALIE:

It's unnecessary.

CHAMPAGNE:

You are mistaken.

ROSALIE:

It doesn't concern me.

CHAMPAGNE:

On the contrary—judge, rather. I begin—you are holder of the Post Nonancourt—that's very fine but it doesn't suffice. You lack harness, you lack fodder, and the stables are falling to ruin. To place your affairs on a suitable footing you need seven to eight thousand pounds.

ROSALIE:

Come off it!

CHAMPAGNE:

Let's say 6,000—So, selling off everything down there at Bar-Le-Duc you picked up less than 1,000 crowns. That's about half—still, your trip and your first expenses to install yourself and they, roughly put a hole in the sum? What's going to happen? An ill equipped post necessarily delays the service. I don't give you six weeks before your commission will be revoked. Once revoked, nothing will remain to you, you'll fall into poverty with all those you support.

ROSALIE:

Those that I support. That's all the same to me. Do you think, I concern myself about others? Why'd you come to tell me all this?

CHAMPAGNE:

To get to politics, and to propose to you to mount your Post in an agreeable manner.

ROSALIE:

Explain yourself.

CHAMPAGNE:

You know about Prince Stanislas since your former inn at Bar-Le-Duc was close to the Château.

ROSALIE:

There and elsewhere—I've heard a lot about him, but I've never seen him.

(Aside) I've only seen his mother, the Queen.

CHAMPAGNE:

You cannot have any personal affection for him.

ROSALIE:

I have none.

CHAMPAGNE:

In that case, we are going to understand each other. This Stanislas will spend tomorrow with you at Nonancourt.

ROSALIE:

How do you know that?

CHAMPAGNE:

Because I've undertaken to arrest him.

ROSALIE:

Ah!—You are—

CHAMPAGNE:

The Prince will reach the coasts of Normandy from where he must embark—Nonancourt is on his route. Besides I can tell you plainly, since you will be one of ours. All the horses here are led by postillons, and all the postillons have orders to head to Nonancourt.

ROSALIE:

All the postillons, in that case, are yours?

CHAMPAGNE:

All!

ROSALIE:

And you were counting on me in advance since you gave me the Post—at Nonancourt.

CHAMPAGNE:

When one has your character, Madame Valentin, one never refuses to make a fortune honestly.

ROSALIE:

Honestly! Man, you are taking me for someone else. I'm not the twin sister of Judas.

CHAMPAGNE:

I take you for what you are—a woman of wit, without prejudices—consider—

ROSALIE:

I have considered—find someone else. It's not for generosity or nobility, at least—It's to sleep peacefully, you understand, I cling to my repose—If I gave a man up, I would have bad dreams.

CHAMPAGNE:

And if, by giving up this man you spared thousands of lives?

ROSALIE:

I'm not clever enough to understand that—your servant, Mr. Champagne.

(She starts to leave)

CHAMPAGNE: (Detaining her)

Briefly—very briefly, I am going to put your finger on the truth. Refuse your fortune, that's your lookout, but to commit an evil deed—

ROSALIE:

An evil deed?

CHAMPAGNE:

A crime, Madame! Prince Stanislas is going to ignite a war throughout Europe.

ROSALIE:

War will even come to Nonancourt?

CHAMPAGNE:

Assuredly.

ROSALIE: (Dreamily)

War! That's how my poor brother died—I recall my poor mother's sobs. And what will be done to this poor young man?

CHAMPAGNE:

What one does with a poor fool, Madame. The gates of Bar-Le-Duc will reopen for him.

ROSALIE:

That's all?

CHAMPAGNE:

That's all.

ROSALIE:

To spare the mourning of so many poor mothers!

CHAMPAGNE:

I didn't mention to you the reward of 10,000 rubles.

ROSALIE:

Ten thousand.

CHAMPAGNE:

In French, 20,000 pounds. Think about what I've told you—soon, I will come to seek your reply.

ROSALIE:

So be it.

CHAMPAGNE: (Aside)

She's one of us.

(Aloud) Till later, Madame Valentin.

(He leaves)

ROSALIE:

Till later, Mr. Champagne!

(Alone) Twenty thousand pounds and I will prevent war in Europe—Why not do a good deed when it brings money?

BONAVENTURE: (Entering, aside)

He left!

ROSALIE:

If I don't do it, someone else will, and, besides for me I have nothing in here (She points to her heart). And I'm not lending anything on it.—The heart is only useful for causing stupidities. I am sure of the arms of Minon, Aunt Catherine, my brother's children, and Bonaventure. Ah, that one works more than he costs me.

BONAVENTURE: (Aside)

Thanks, Boss-Lady.

ROSALIE: (Continuing)

Well, I will give 10,000 pounds to Minon, to get married—with Bonaventure, if she likes.

BONAVENTURE: (Aside)

Again! Thanks, Boss-Lady.

ROSALIE: (Continuing)

I'll give 5,000 pounds to Aunt Catherine so as not to listen to her weep over her poverty—that irritates me—and I will place 5,000 pounds for the children.

BONAVENTURE: (Advancing)

Ten plus five are fifteen plus five are twenty.

ROSALIE:

Right, you were actually there?

BONAVENTURE:

You've really got lots of money, Boss-Lady.

ROSALIE:

I have 20,000 pounds.

BONAVENTURE:

Where are you getting them from?

ROSALIE:

In the end I have them.

BONAVENTURE:

So much the better! But take twenty from twenty—there remains zero.

ROSALIE:

Yes, but I will be rid of all these people. You see plainly I am thinking only of myself.

BONAVENTURE: (Aside)

If it's possible to boast like this.

ROSALIE:

Minon, you see, bothers me by being around me. I love her too much—it's over, I no longer want that. Aunt Catherine, hell, an old woman who raised you. The kids, my poor brother Benoît dead quite young—he had a brave heart—One cannot treat them roughly as one would like, you know that very well—one must use gloves. Holy God! Once I no longer have Minon, nor aunt, nor the children—

BONAVENTURE:

You will miss them, Boss-Lady.

ROSALIE:

I will be free like they are and weigh less than a feather—

(Rising) Come on, it's agreed—so much the worse for Prince Stanislas.

BONAVENTURE:

Huh? Prince Stanislas?

ROSALIE:

You won't understand anything about it. It's over your head. Hey! Waiters! Waiters! We are going to leave at night. Call our postillons—and have them hitch up the carriage and be quick about it.

BONAVENTURE:

Yes, Boss-Lady.

(The servants of the Inn enter)

ROSALIE:

Wait, Bonaventure, you are going to show the maid how to heat my double slippers. Do you have my fur cape? The blanket to put on my legs? Ah, ah—I must have my comforts my mother didn't. The blanket to put on my legs—maid! You'll keep my sugared wine very hot with a little cinnamon. That gives strength.

BONAVENTURE:

That puts new life into you, Boss-Lady.

ROSALIE:

Get going—and be quick about it. Decidedly so much the worse for Prince Stanislas. Heavens! Everybody! Here we are with our lazy postillons.

BONAVENTURE:

One would say they are bringing in a wounded man.

(JOLIBOIS and postillons carry in Stanislas in their arms. He's pale and his clothes are in disorder)

ROSALIE:

What's this?

JOLIBOIS:

A poor young man that we found wounded on the edge of the forest.

ROSALIE:

That's fine—place him under the porch. And what about the carriage, my lazy bones—this doesn't concern us.

STANISLAS:

Madame—a word, I beg you.

ROSALIE:

With me?—I don't know you.

STANISLAS:

Make these brave folks withdraw. I want to speak to you—to you alone.

ROSALIE:

I don't have the time.

STANISLAS:

Listen to me—it's a question of life and death.

ROSALIE: (To others)

Move away (the group around STANISLAS recoils)

JOLIBOIS:

The Boss-Lady is going to give him a dressing down.

SERVING GIRL:

She's a bitch, that woman.

ROSALIE: (To STANISLAS)

What's this your babbling to me about?—what question of life and death? Whose?

STANISLAS:

Mine, Madame, mine only. I am a foreigner, pursued—wounded—my strength is at an end.

ROSALIE:

All vagabonds say as much (abruptly taking his hands). You have a fever.

STANISLAS:

I'm hurting, Madame. I beg you, hide me—don't give me up.

ROSALIE: (Aside)

He's quite young—He's trembling. His shirt's all bloody.

(Aloud) Lean on me.

STANISLAS:

I had escaped, but I wanted to hug my mother one last time.

ROSALIE:

His mother? Some deserter! Cold pierces him to his bones—this poor boy.

(The postillons hasten to make preparations for departure)

ROSALIE: (To BONAVENTURE)

My fur cloak?

BONAVENTURE:

Here it is, Boss-Lady.

ROSALIE:

Wrap him in it.

BONAVENTURE:

Him? And you?

ROSALIE:

No back talk.

STANISLAS:

Oh, thanks, Madame.

ROSALIE:

Shut up!

SERVING GIRL:

Here's your sugar wine, Madame.

ROSALIE:

Fine—you, drink this!

(She gives the wine to STANISLAS, who hesitates)

Come on.

(Softly) It will warm up your heart. Bring the carriage around. You—Boute-Entrain, come take this lad there—gently. Gently—I told you gently!

STANISLAS:

How can I show you my gratitude, Madame?

ROSALIE:

By shutting up. It will tire you to speak.

(She coddles STANISLAS as they take him out. The carriage appears behind the Inn)

You are going to cram him in my place—on the back—and you'll place the cushion….

BONAVENTURE: (Angrily)

And you?

ROSALIE:

No back talk!

(She helps place Stanislas in the carriage)

If he makes an outcry—watch out. Holy God—what rough hands you have. There—at last. There. He is in his place.

CHAMPAGNE: (Emerging from the Inn)

One doesn't dine badly in Saint Germain—Ah! There you are, dear lady—well?

ROSALIE:

Well, we are in agreement. So much the worse for Prince Stanislas.

CHAMPAGNE:

In that case, hasten to leave, the Prince is perhaps already en route.

ROSALIE:

Mount, Bonaventure.

(To CHAMPAGNE) Don't worry, my horses are good.

CHAMPAGNE:

He'll be at your place before dawn.

ROSALIE:

We will be there to receive him.

(She climbs in)

And his business is done.

CHAMPAGNE:

Bon Voyage! He must not escape us.

ROSALIE:

To whom are you talking? I want my 20,000 pounds. Whip, coachman.

(She gives a tap of the whip, the carriage moves forward. Speaking to CHAMPAGNE)

Take care of yourself.

CURTAIN

ACT IV

The Inn of the Post at Nonancourt.

An eating table. A small round table near with a spindle nearby.

MINON: (Alone, knitting, beside the round table)

The day yesterday seemed long to me—longer—it's because my sister Rosalie was absent. Oh, yes, that's why.

(She puts down her knitting and crosses her hands on her knees)

Was it for that? Wasn't I thinking of him more often than of my sister Rosalie?

(She picks up a book of hours on the round table)

When I was little, I went to the prettiest letter in my book of hours to know if the weather would be good in holidays. Suppose I pull the most beautiful letter to know? To know what? I must be crazy.

(She takes a pen from her corsage. She puts down the book.)

Let's see, first of all for no—if he doesn't love—well—I am out of trouble (solemnly) to the right for no.

(She sticks her pen in the side of the book and opens it. ANDRÉ appears in the doorway and remains motionless)

MINON: (Looking at the page)

The first letter is an A.

(She pulls, ANDRÉ comes quietly behind her)

ANDRÉ: (Looking at the page over her shoulder)

An A.—Amours!

MINON: (Rising with a start)

Oh! How you frightened me. You were listening to me. Fie! How bad that is!

ANDRÉ:

I come—

MINON:

To dare to speak to me of love.

ANDRÉ:

Wasn't me; it was the book—the dear little book. Ah! Minon! Miss! Do you actually have the heart to Scold me? And shouldn't I rather be the one reproaching you? To suspect me, to question the book?

MINON:

Heck, you've never said anything to me, Mr. André.

ANDRÉ:

And, the way I looked at you, if I didn't speak?

MINON:

I understood it—a little bit, because I advised my sister Rosalie not to receive you—

ANDRÉ:

Naughty—

MINON:

Speak to me frankly, Mr. André—Is it for me that you've assumed this costume?

ANDRÉ:

Minon—I don't know how to lie—

MINON: (Angrily)

Then it wasn't for me!

ANDRÉ:

No—it wasn't for you. It was a question of saving a proscribed man. Whose head has a price on it.

MINON:

Ah, good God! And why?

ANDRÉ:

Because he is a Prince.

MINON:

Ah—the one whose father was King of Poland?

ANDRÉ:

That's it.

MINON:

Is this possible, I've spoken to a Prince! Moreover, it wasn't for me that you escaped from the Post, yesterday, Mr. André—and that you remained outside all during the day, and the night?

ANDRÉ:

I went to Saint Germain, where my duty called me.

MINON:

Hold on—are you going to tell me you are not a gentleman?

ANDRÉ:

I am one.

MINON:

My little book.

(She places the book on the table)

We will no longer concern ourselves with Mr. André who is a gentleman. Gentlemen don't marry poor girls like me—Your servant, Mr. André.

(She starts to leave)

ANDRÉ: (Stopping her)

Minon! Stay, I beg you! Are you punishing me for having spoken without artifice? I've just given you proof that I don't know how to lie. Listen to me and trust me! My name is noble, it's true; but my father and my mother are dead, I am alone. Misfortune makes me free. In this would I have only my sword. Minon, I love you sincerely and honestly. I swear to you that in my poor house you will be honored as a queen and happier than a queen can be down here. But I tell you this, if you don't wish to be my wife I am a soldier. I will say goodbye to you, I will wish you happiness—and I will say goodbye to you forever.

(Pause) You don't respond? Must I leave?

MINON:

Ah, a noise of horses. It's my sister already! Ah! Lord God. Nothing's been prepared. I'm going to be scolded.

ANDRÉ:

Minon!—a word—just one word.

MINON: (At the window)

There are three men—I know them. All of them came to Bar-Le-Duc. The first is the one who got the commission for my sister.

ANDRÉ:

I did that!

MINON:

You! Indeed, there were two.

ANDRÉ:

I want to see who got the other one.

(Aside) Champagne, the henchman of the Dutchman! Robin and Morel—my two traitors. And the Prince is going to come.

MINON:

One of the two others (recoiling). It's him.

ANDRÉ:

Well?

MINON: (In a choked voice)

He's the man who remained alone in the lower hall of the White Horse Inn—The day Papa Valentin was murdered in his bed.

ANDRÉ: (Aside)

Robin! They all were there.

(Aloud) Today's like that day, Minon—it's a question of assassination.

MINON: (Shocked)

What are you saying?

ANDRÉ:

I'm withdrawing; these men must not see me.

MINON:

They know you?

ANDRÉ:

They know me—and I shan't lose sight of them.

(He leaves)

MINON: (Alone for a moment)

Lord God—I no longer have blood in my veins—and my sister Rosalie isn't here. Here they come!

CHAMPAGNE: (Entering)

Hello—pretty girl.

ROBIN:

Hello, Minette!

MOREL:

A love like this child!

MINON: (Very upset)

Gentlemen—

CHAMPAGNE:

Must we complain of the Post of Nonancourt?

(She wants to leave)

Hold on, my pretty baby—! Are we frightening you?

MINON:

Oh, no, gentlemen. No, surely.

CHAMPAGNE:

The Boss-Lady isn't going to be late getting here, I think?

MINON:

No—we are expecting her from one moment to the next.

CHAMPAGNE:

And tell me—the postillon, André?

MINON: (Aside)

They know he's here!

CHAMPAGNE:

That gives you beautiful color, pretty baby, when I speak of André.

MINON:

He's not in the house, Sir.

CHAMPAGNE: (Aside to his men)

I told you he's in Saint-Germain with the Prince.

(To MINON, who's squirming) One moment, my dear child—what the devil!

MINON: (Curtsying and leaving)

Excuse me, gentlemen. I'm going to my work.

(Aside) Oh—these men. Perhaps they intend to murder André!

(She leaves)

CHAMPAGNE:

We have to occupy ourselves with this child.

ROBIN:

Truly!

MOREL:

It's nice work! Really.

CHAMPAGNE:

But first of all, how many are you around Nonancourt?

ROBIN:

A dozen, counting ourselves. There are as many ambushes set up on the road to Saint Germain.

CHAMPAGNE:

Listen to me—on the subject of the little one….

ROBIN:

Ah! Ah!

CHAMPAGNE:

The Boss wants her.

ROBIN:

To do the honors of the little house?

MOREL:

It's all very simple; he's got what it takes, that man.

CHAMPAGNE:

She must be carried off tonight and leave with you for Paris.

ROBIN:

Agreed.

MOREL:

The Boss pays well.

CHAMPAGNE:

He's going to come. You'll have your wages. Now to your work. Don't let anything happen on the trip, understand!

ROBIN: (Rising)

That goes without saying.

CHAMPAGNE:

Except, of course, the chair of the Boss—and the carriage of the Boss-Lady.

ROBIN: (Aside)

Stop the carriage of that woman? I'd prefer to attack the devil!

MOREL:

When, for the little one?

CHAMPAGNE:

At dusk by the rear gate.

ROBIN:

And we'll be paid?

CHAMPAGNE:

In advance—go!

ROBIN and MOREL:

We'll be there.

CHAMPAGNE:

How was the Prince able to escape from Saint Germain? It's inexplicable!

(Calling) Hey, someone!

(A servant enters)

A room—I'm falling asleep.

SERVANT:

I'm going to escort you.

CHAMPAGNE:

Wake me as soon as Madame Valentin returns.

SERVANT:

Suffice, Sir.

CHAMPAGNE:

When one's ridden hell-for-leather all night….

(He passes in front of the servant and leaves)

ANDRÉ: (At the door at the right)

Psst!

(The servant stops)

Under no pretext will you wake him.

SERVANT:

Because?

ANDRÉ: (Grasping his hand hard)

Because if you wake him, I will break your bones.

SERVANT: (Pulling back his hurt hand)

Fine, Mr. André, fine.

(Aside) What a grip.

(He leaves, shaking his hand)

ANDRÉ: (Alone for a moment)

Twelve men, posted around Nonancourt! They intend to kidnap Minon. How to protect her against their shameful plot while accomplishing my oath?—Because I've sworn not to abandon the Prince until he's set foot on his vessel.

MINON: (Entering, followed by servants of both sexes. She's very agitated)

How can you think of remaining here? My sister is arriving.

ANDRÉ:

We have time to exchange some words—something terrible is shaping up. For pity for yourself, come.

MINON:

Speak to my sister.

ANDRÉ:

I cannot.

(Aside) Her sister. She's sold out to our enemies.

(Aloud) In heaven's name, listen to me.

MINON:

Not a word. To your horses, Mr. André, my sister's here.

ANDRÉ: (To himself)

Oh. I won't leave her in the hands of these wretches. I will save her at all costs.

(Exit ANDRÉ)

(The servants make way to let the Boss-Lady pass).

ROSALIE: (Entering, in the wings)

Prepare the best bed in the house.

MINON: (Rushing to her)

Are you ill, Sis?

ROSALIE: (To servants)

Hello! Hello! Warm the best bed in the inn.

BONAVENTURE:

You heard her. Warm the best bed in the inn.

ROSALIE:

You shut up. Isn't it enough to say it once? You'd think it's a question of a prince.

BONAVENTURE:

Hell, Boss-Lady!

ROSALIE:

For a famished vagabond that fell in my arms! As if I didn't have enough people to take care of! Holy God! These things happen only to me.

BONAVENTURE:

You coddled him so much and doted on him the whole trip!

ROSALIE:

The better he's cared for, the sooner he'll be cured. The sooner he's cured, the sooner I'll be rid of him.

MINON:

She's really in a bad mood!

(Aloud) Sis, in that case, it's not for you?

ROSALIE:

Hello, little Sis. I didn't see you. (Sits down) Nothing new here?

MINON:

Sis!

(aside) I don't dare tell her about these men.

ROSALIE: (Pointing to MINON)

Look at this little girl here. Always trembling before me. Wouldn't you say she'd been beaten?

(She turns her back on her and goes to sit at the table)

(To BONAVENTURE) What did I tell you? Aunt Catherine was there—on the front steps. On occasions like these she finds her legs work.

BONAVENTURE:

To come kiss you, Boss-Lady.

ROSALIE:

Leave me alone! If I hadn't brought something for her you would have seen.

BONAVENTURE: (Aside)

Old folks—They don't dislike sweets.

ROSALIE:

The children come to throw themselves in my arms.

BONAVENTURE:

Poor little loves.

ROSALIE:

There was one who was feeling in my left pocket.

BONAVENTURE:

Jean-Baptiste, my godson.

ROSALIE:

Another one who felt in my right pocket.

BONAVENTURE:

Nicholas, my godson.

ROSALIE:

Another in front of me.

BONAVENTURE:

Charlotte, my goddaughter. Before becoming a confidential servant, I was godfather of all these children.

ROSALIE:

Come here, Minon—There's nothing for you, you know.

MINON:

What do I need, Sis?

ROSALIE:

Well answered—already a hypocritical little slut.

BONAVENTURE:

Ah, Boss-Lady, for goodness sakes—

ROSALIE:

No one's talking to you—You always support her, by Jove!

MINON:

Sis, who is that man—that vagabond, as you say—and that you had carried gently, quite gently….

ROSALIE:

A stupid act of mine! Let's not talk about it!

(MINON kisses her hand, ROSALIE pulls her hand away)

I'm not in the mood for caresses! Go away, Bonaventure—I have to scold this child—Watch over that young vagabond—a bouillon, a chicken wing, whatever.

BONAVENTURE:

So long as it's good, right, Boss-Lady?

ROSALIE:

You will come inform me when this Mr. Champagne and his boss arrive.

BONAVENTURE:

Don't scold her too much.

ROSALIE: (Rudely)

Get out of here!

BONAVENTURE:

Yes, Boss-Lady.

(He leaves terrified)

MINON: (Aside)

Scold me! Can she suspect?

ROSALIE:

Now, the two of us are alone, Miss Minon I'm not pleased with you.

MINON: (Aside)

She knows everything.

ROSALIE:

This has got to end.

MINON: (Trembling)

Sis—

ROSALIE:

Fine! Fine! Today, I'm not going to be caught with your cajolery—I'm very mad.

MINON: (Aside)

Ah, my God.

ROSALIE:

This has got to end, I tell you. All these dresses, all these hairdos—all these baubles—in a word, it doesn't suit me at all.

MINON: (Sighing in relief, aside)

Ah! How afraid I was.

(Aloud) My darling sister, I will dress as you like.

ROSALIE: (Mockingly)

Ah, no doubt, no doubt—you are obedient,—in words—you never revolt—but end by doing your little will. Go away, you are worth neither more nor less than the others. Where were your dresses made?

MINON:

At Bar-Le-Duc.

ROSALIE:

The idiot! She left a fold in the back. She's really lucky that we've left the country. I would have changed it. But look here, in conscience—is this shirt made for a girl in an inn!—For you are only a waiter in an inn, Minon.

MINON: (Sighing)

I know that well enough, Sis.

ROSALIE:

Yes, yes—you sigh hugely, my beauty. You prefer to have been picked up by a princess—I conceive that—

MINON: (Tearfully)

Oh, my Sis—

ROSALIE:

If you cry, we are going to get angry. Dry your eyes, Inn girl—Inn girl—there are inns and inns. I told you to dry your eyes

(She dries MINON's eyes with her apron)

The Post of Nonancourt—Holy God—If someone besides me were going to call you an Inn girl….

MINON:

It's still the truth.

ROSALIE:

Not at all! That is to say—in the end, no question, but I don't intend to be dishonest with you. They will give it to the Inn girls like that. You're a flirt.-Great misfortune—Come on, smile at me—Better than that! It's your age. And yet, coquette, let's understand each other.

(She caresses MINON's hair) As for me, I did my hair better than this—and it was never as beautiful—and I wasn't a flirt! Are you still angry with me?

MINON:

Is that possible?

ROSALIE:

I am going to speak to you as if to a great, but quite reasonable, young lady. One can scold you for baubles but actually you don't have baubles and, besides, I find these people amusing! When the baubles that one has are not owed to anyone—hell—right, little girl? What was it they said? Pull that kerchief out a little so I can see it, Minette.

MINON:

My kerchief, Sis? Do you find it too good looking? It's simple linen.

ROSALIE: (Showing her a kerchief that she's pulled from under her cloak)

Do you prefer this one?

MINON:

Oh! Charming embroidery.

ROSALIE:

Try it, would you, Minon?

MINON: (Trying the kerchief)

I really want to.

(ROSALIE goes to unhook a mirror and places it before her)

It's very pretty. It's actually very pretty.

ROSALIE:

Is there something prettier than you?

(Admiring her)

Do you know that you have the neck of a Duchess, Minon? You need a necklace on that neck.

MINON:

A necklace!

ROSALIE:

You know perfectly well—I promised you to replace that chain and that medal. Don't budge.

(She attaches a necklace)

MINON:

A pearl necklace!

ROSALIE:

If you jump about like that, how am I going to fasten it?

MINON: (Looking at herself)

What joy!

ROSALIE:

Little crazy-head! But I'm more of a child than you.

MINON: (Tenderly)

Ah! Sis! Sis! How sweet you are! How good you are!

ROSALIE:

Me? As for me I'm always scolding you.

(MINON covers her with kisses)

I'm wrong to scold you, poor darling angel! You don't have a mother. You need someone better to love you. How pretty she is. (Passionately) How beautiful she is.

(Getting hold of herself) You understand plainly, Minette, that I find you pretty—because I am your sister—almost your mother. If the popinjays tell you this, you mustn't believe them. I'd like to know if you love me, Minon.

MINON:

Oh, Sis! I cannot tell you. I owe you everything.

ROSALIE:

You owe me nothing, child. You are the happiness and the calm of my youth. You owe me nothing, and I owe you everything—if you love me.

MINON:

If I love you? Why, I am your work! I am your daughter.

ROSALIE:

That's true, thanks. Do you know, Minon, now, here you are big and beautiful—I intend to marry you young—so you'll be happy for a long while.

MINON: (Frightened)

Me get married, Sis?

ROSALIE:

Don't worry—I will choose for you. You will have a dowry. Ten thousand pounds.

MINON: (Aside)

If I told her—

ROSALIE: (Pulling her suddenly to her breast)

Let me hug you well as I ought.

(Suddenly pushing her away) Heavens, little girl, I love you too much! That's not common sense. I couldn't love you so much if I was your real mother. If something happened to you, I would die.

MINON:

Die!

ROSALIE: (Laughing and changing tone)

I said that—and you believe me. Die! Plague! As if we were going to do it. When one goes about, twiddling sensibility like this. Holy God! Let's laugh, Minon! Come bring my spindle, take your embroidery

(They sit by the round table)

ROSALIE: What have you done during my absence?

MINON: (Aside)

So much the worse! She's in a good mood. I'm going to risk it.

(Aloud) Marie-Rose came to see me.

ROSALIE: (Knitting)

Ah—the neighbor with scandals.

MINON: (Knitting)

She told me a very touching story.

ROSALIE:

I'm wary of touching stories.

MINON:

Oh—this one….

ROSALIE:

Some idle talk. Let's hear her story.

MINON:

There was once a very pretty girl hereabouts….

ROSALIE:

Not as pretty as you.

MINON:

…Who lived with her mother, who was quite nice. But not as nice as you—that's impossible.

ROSALIE:

You'll give me money for my work—that's good.

MINON:

And a young noble who loved the young girl.

ROSALIE:

Ah! Where?

MINON:

If you don't want me to tell the tale, Sis….

ROSALIE:

Keep going.

MINON:

It's not very long. The young lord came to work in the house like a keeper and then the mother noticed that he wasn't an ordinary game keeper—and then….

ROSALIE:

And then?

MINON:

Tell me—what would you have done in the mother's place?

ROSALIE:

What did the mother in your story do?

MINON:

The mother married them.

ROSALIE:

As for me, I'd put the gallant in prison and I'd put the pretty girl in prison.

MINON: (Aside)

Ah, my God!

ROSALIE: (Rising)

And I forbid you to receive this Marie-Rose.

MINON: (Aside)

Prison for him—The convent for me!

ROSALIE: (Aside)

Why'd she tell me this story?

(To BONAVENTURE who enters) What is it you want?

BONAVENTURE:

It's the folks from Paris. The man and the woman that I took the umbrella from. They are in the court—and that's not all. There's the young vagabond.

ROSALIE:

Well?

BONAVENTURE:

Well—As soon as he saw them he became very pale.

ROSALIE:

What do you want me to do about that?

BONAVENTURE: (To ROSALIE)

He wants to see you—in private.

ROSALIE:

Let him come.

(to MINON) Go, little girl.

MINON:

Sis!

ROSALIE:

There you go trembling again! I'm not mad at you for your story, but go, will you! I need to be alone.

(She kisses her)

(MINON leaves and STANISLAS enters)

(Aside) Once again busy with others.

(Aloud) (To STANISLAS) What do you want?

STANISLAS:

You saved my life, Madame.

ROSALIE:

I know that well enough.

STANISLAS:

To complete your kindness, give me the means to flee.

ROSALIE:

Why flee? You are safe here with me.

STANISLAS:

Just now, I noticed in the courtyard—

ROSALIE:

The Dutchman and his wife? Don't worry, these folks are not coming for you. They are after bigger game.

STANISLAS:

Madame.

ROSALIE:

They after Prince Stanislas of Poland—(Laughing) And you are a Prince, are you?

STANISLAS:

I am Prince Stanislas of Poland, Madame.

BONAVENTURE:

The vagabond—! He's—

ROSALIE: (Recoiling)

You are—Now there's a story.

(Aloud) So much the worse for you, young man. You would have done better not to tell me that.

BONAVENTURE:

Why's that, Boss-Lady?

STANISLAS:

Gentlemen like us, Madame, speak the truth even in the face of death.

ROSALIE: (Aside)

Still, he doesn't seem to be mad or furious.

(Aloud) If I had known yesterday you were this firebrand of discord, this unchained lion—I don't recall the exact words of Mr. Champagne, but I know what I said—

STANISLAS:

Madame—I want only one thing—to cure the wounds of my country.

ROSALIE:

That's it. You are more gentle than a lamb.

STANISLAS:

Every sovereign is a soldier—especially amongst us, the scepter is a sword. Madame, it's heaven that punishes the earth with the great flail of battles. Once out of its scabbard my sword won't go back in until it's victorious.

ROSALIE:

Hell, where one has only jumped a moat—right, Bonaventure.

BONAVENTURE:

Moat?—by Jove—Boss-Lady….

(Aside) I don't understand anything of this.

ROSALIE: (Aside)

But he won't cajole me. Ah, indeed, for goodness sakes!

(Aloud) This queen who is down here in Saint Germain—

STANISLAS:

She's my mother.

ROSALIE:

Do you know what she did to me—your mother?

BONAVENTURE:

Yikes! The seven crown dress.

STANISLAS:

I don't know, Madame, but I recall that you passed on the route. As for me, I was in the woods. At that moment, I was sending my mother a final kiss. She made her carriage turn so as to see me one moment more.

ROSALIE: (Moved)

Poor woman!

(To BONAVENTURE) My dress had a bad tint.

BONAVENTURE:

And besides, it doesn't look well on you—Boss-Lady.

ROSALIE:

All that is well and good, but it's not a reason to set fire to the four corners of the universe. What have you to reply to that?

STANISLAS:

They know you are generous and good. They couldn't turn you against me except by deceiving you. I hate war as much as you can detest it. If I make war, the first blood which will spill will emerge from my veins, and this blood will only redden the earth of my country. It's there we shall fight, Madame, it's there we shall die—it's there the last of my men will fall, if God doesn't give us victory—for the war I shall fight, Madame, is a just war—it's a holy war—it's the war of a nation in arms to repulse a foreigner.

ROSALIE:

Why that's fine—isn't it, Bonaventure?.

BONAVENTURE:

I really do think it's fine. Almost makes you want to be a soldier—

STANISLAS:

Madame, I've shown you the bottom of my heart. Will you give me the means of rejoining my friends who are waiting for me at the sea shore at the Inn of The Black Head at Quilleboeuf?

BONAVENTURE:

Listen!

ROSALIE:

That's them.

(STANISLAS takes a step to sneak out by the door on the left. ROSALIE stops him abruptly)

Where are you going? Those men who are arriving promised me 20,000 if I delivered you to them.

BONAVENTURE:

20,000 pounds! Ah, Bah! That's where you got them….

STANISLAS: (Standing up)

And you didn't refuse. Well, give me up, then! I am ready. I'll die as a Prince.

ROSALIE:

It's true. Look, Bonaventure—he's not afraid. He's a noble young man.

CORNIL: (Outside)

He's here. We are going to take him like a wolf in a trap.

ROSALIE:

It's the voice of the Dutchman. We have no time to consider. Ah, that way!

(She opens a small door on the right)

Go in with him, Bonaventure!

BONAVENTURE:

But….

ROSALIE:

No buts! Listen to me. If you love me, you will find a way to save him.

BONAVENTURE: (With enthusiasm)

If I love you!

STANISLAS: (To ROSALIE)

Excellent and generous heart!

ROSALIE: (Pushing them)

There they come—Holy God!

(They leave. Just as STANISLAS vanishes, CORNIL appears in the doorway. ROSALIE is standing before the door as if she wanted to defend it.)

CORNIL:

I am positive of it, I saw him!

(Haughtily, advancing towards ROSALIE)

Madame, is there someone hidden in that room?

ROSALIE:

Yes.

CORNIL:

Who is it?

ROSALIE:

That's none of your business.

CORNIL:

My men are around—I'm seeking someone worth two millions. All this is my business.

ROSALIE:

I am mistress in my own home, perhaps.

CORNIL:

In your home! It's through me that this is your home—

ROSALIE:

Take back what you've given me, but you shall not enter there.

CORNIL:

I will enter, I shall enter, I tell you, if we have to force this door. Follow me! Get back, Madame! The Prince is there—

WIFE: (Entering)

The Prince!

BONAVENTURE: (Appearing in the doorway with the clothes of STANISLAS)

I'm here—what do you want with me?

ROSALIE: (Astonished)

Him!

CORNIL:

The Prince.

ROSALIE: (Low to BONAVENTURE)

Has he left?

BONAVENTURE:

I don't know.

(CORNIL's men enter tumultuously and in arms)

CHAMPAGNE: (Entering)

What's all this uproar? And that Post Chaise, hitched up in the Court?

ROSALIE: (To BONAVENTURE)

We are lost!

CORNIL:

That's my Post Chaise, Mr. Champagne. Ah, ah—you are a clever man—and I was very good to pay so dearly for your services when I myself am doing your work.

CHAMPAGNE:

What do you mean?

CORNIL:

You are seeking the Prince and as for me, I found him—

CHAMPAGNE: (Astonished)

The Prince!

CORNIL: (Pointing to BONAVENTURE)

There he is, by Jove.

CHAMPAGNE:

That's not him, listen—there's treachery—that's not him.

(Noise of the Post chaise and the whip of the Postillon)

BONAVENTURE:

Gone!

ROSALIE:

Saved!

JOLIBOIS: (Rushing into the room)

Boss-Lady, your two trusty men—André and Bonaventure….

ROSALIE:

Well.

JOLIBOIS:

They just left with Miss Minon.

ROSALIE:

With Minon!

JOLIBOIS:

In the Post Chaise!

CORNIL:

In mine?

CHAMPAGNE: (Seizing him by the collar)

Here's Bonaventure!

JOLIBOIS:

My, my—and the other one.

CHAMPAGNE: (To ROSALIE)

You grasp everything, Madame—The other one is the Prince. The Prince who undertakes himself to avenge us and punish you. The handsome postillon André is his damned soul. He's the Chevalier de Rieux who's carrying off your sister!

ROSALIE: (Altered)

My sister! Minon! Ruined! Ruined! And it's this André. I have done good again, and again. I'm punished for it, listen you, I'm going to do wrong, here!—And I bet I'll be rewarded for it.

BONAVENTURE: (Trying to stop her)

Boss-Lady, be careful.

ROSALIE:

Leave me alone!

(To CHAMPAGNE) You want to follow his track? He's going straight to Quilleboeuf—he'll not stop until he gets to the Black Head Inn.

CHAMPAGNE:

Thanks, Lady! Let's be on our way, Boss.

CORNIL:

I am ready.

CHAMPAGNE:

We will get to Quilleboeuf first—I'm the one who says so. And this time, dead or alive, we've got him.

(CHAMPAGNE, CORNIL, and the wife leave hurriedly)

BONAVENTURE: (As ROSALIE lets herself fall in a chair)

What have you done?

ROSALIE:

I've done well.

BONAVENTURE:

They are going to catch him.

ROSALIE:

So much the better. Doing good for evil belongs to angels. Good for good—Evil for evil.—That's our law and we are not saints. But to render ill for good, that's hell down here—Let them take him, let them kill him, let them do what they wish with him! Minon! My darling little Minon—Do you know how I loved her?—Who knew?—Did I know myself? Ah, she was my heart, all my heart! Minon!—My sister, my daughter.

BONAVENTURE:

Boss-Lady.

ROSALIE:

Well?

BONAVENTURE:

The two men who were at the White Horse Inn, the day when your father was killed, march in the entourage of this Champagne.

ROSALIE:

Assassins!

BONAVENTURE:

And it's you who set them on his trail.

ROSALIE:

It's me.

(Covering her face with her hands)

(Abruptly)

Have my two best horses saddled.

BONAVENTURE:

To do what?

ROSALIE:

I want to repair what I did.

BONAVENTURE:

To leave yourself? What are you thinking, Boss-Lady? There must be danger—

ROSALIE:

Who cares!

BONAVENTURE:

They're assassins.

ROSALIE:

You'll take pistols.

(She puts her cape over her shoulders)

BONAVENTURE:

It's well enough for me, Madame. I'm a man—but you—Boss-Lady, a woman!

ROSALIE:

A woman who has no fear is as good as a man. And as for me, I've never been afraid. So, I tell you.

(She pulls him toward the door) You'll take pistols—and the care of God!

CURTAIN

ACT V

The Black Head Inn at Quilleboeuf.

A gallery at the back; behind it ships can be seen at anchor.

CHAMPAGNE: (Alone, writing at a table on which are two pistols)

I would never have believed that this little Prince Stanislas could lead me so far! But who cares! My last role is won in advance. Long live great means!

(He writes) One is happy in truth, to have made a bit of something in one's life. If I hadn't been valet de Chamber to the revenue farmer of the Hermitage, who counterfeited so perfectly, the signature of the comptroller I would probably be unaware of this ingenious art of making people speak without their being aware of it—(he puts down his pen) Because I was a valet de Chamber and worse than that! I think I received some blows with a cane! (Rubs his shoulder) I'm quite sure of it.

(Taking up his pen) Son of a bitch! My lackeys better watch out when I become a millionaire. I know from experience how one roughs up the knaves.

(writing, looking at his papers) There—I'd almost be fooled by it myself. The Lieutenant of Police couldn't imitate his own signature better.

(Takes the pistols) And this? Is it in working order?

(He pulls his powder-flash and charges his pistols) Hey! Somebody!

(He hides the pistols under his clothes) My friend, Champagne—you are risking your neck this time. Hang on to your cards and play carefully!

INNKEEPER:

Here I am, Sir—

CHAMPAGNE:

The tide is low?

INNKEEPER: (At the window)

It's low.

CHAMPAGNE: (Pointing to the port)

At what time can one of these boats sail?

INNKEEPER:

Is it going far?

CHAMPAGNE:

Replies only, friend, and no questions.

INNKEEPER:

We are in dead water—we have to wait the high tide—towards two in the afternoon, maybe, we can set sail.

CHAMPAGNE:

That's fine.

INNKEEPER:

Is that all you wish, Sir—

CHAMPAGNE:

No, I want to know if there is a Judge, a bailiff, a provost—something at least in this little country—

INNKEEPER:

What do you mean little country? The city of Quilleboeuf.

CHAMPAGNE:

Friend, I'm asking you if there's a judge, a provost, a bailiff.

INNKEEPER:

We've got them all here, Sir—and the bailiff is lunching right now in the dining room—if you want to see him.

CHAMPAGNE:

I don't go looking for bailiffs, my lad—bailiffs come to find me.

INNKEEPER: (Aside)

Plague! This is a great person.

CHAMPAGNE:

Go tell him to come—and be quick about it.

INNKEEPER:

Suffice, milord.

(He leaves)

CHAMPAGNE: (Alone)

At two o'clock high tide. We've got time.

INNKEEPER: (Bringing the bailiff)

Trust me, demand his papers—

(He leaves)

BAILIFF:

Sir—

CHAMPAGNE:

You are the bailiff of Quilleboeuf?

BAILIFF: (Proudly)

I have that honor, Sir—and I'd like to know—

CHAMPAGNE:

Have you heard of Abbé-Dubois, the best friend of the Regent—?

BAILIFF:

I should say so! Would you kindly tell me…?

CHAMPAGNE:

Do you know who the best friend of the Abbé-Dubois is?

BAILIFF:

No—but in advance I am his zealous servant, sir, with all my heart—Be so obliging as to—

CHAMPAGNE:

Do you know the signature of the Lieutenant of Police?

BAILIFF:

Sir, I know it. It's my job—and I venerate it. It's my opinion. But that doesn't stop me from asking you—

CHAMPAGNE: (Presenting a paper to him)

Read this.

BAILIFF: (Putting on his glasses)

"Order to Support and blindly obey Mynheer CORNIL VAN ZUYP."

(Looking at Champagne through his glasses)

That name seems to have a foreign ring to it.

CHAMPAGNE:

It's the name of a Dutchman who possesses twenty-eight merchant vessels in the Indian Ocean, three counting houses in Europe, five factories in Bengal, a dozen dwellings in The Antilles, fisheries in Saint-Pierre and Miquelon, etc., etc., etc.

BAILIFF:

This must be a Dutchman comfortably off.

CHAMPAGNE:

He's the best friend of Abbé Dubois—who's the best friend of the Regent.

BAILIFF:

I repeat to you, sir. I am his servant with all my heart. Is it you…?

CHAMPAGNE:

No—but I am his right arm and his factotum.

BAILIFF:

The order is positive. Command, sir, command—the Bailiff of Quilleboeuf has always included obedience in the rank of his virtues.

CHAMPAGNE:

Mynheer Cornil is going to come.

BAILIFF:

In his own person, Sir?

CHAMPAGNE:

With the Countess Pfaffenhoffen, his wife.

BAILIFF:

With his own wife, sir—

CHAMPAGNE:

As noble as he is rich—the last offshoot of the Counts of Pfaffenhoffen—cousin German of the sovereign Prince of Lippe-Rottembourg.

BAILIFF:

Ah, what an honor, sir, for the city of Quilleboeuf.

CHAMPAGNE:

Render yourself worthy of this honor.—They are pursuing fugitives—a prisoner of state.

BAILIFF:

I've understood, sir.

CHAMPAGNE: (Confidentially)

Prince Stanislas of Poland and his accomplices.

BAILIFF:

Hush! Sir, I've understood!

CHAMPAGNE:

Two young men and a young girl.

BAILIFF:

A young girl and two young men—Sir, I've understood.

CHAMPAGNE:

If these fugitives arrive first—

BAILIFF:

In chains, sir.

CHAMPAGNE:

That's it, Mr. Bailiff—They shall learn in Paris that you are an intelligent man.

BAILIFF:

Energetic and sober, sir—and who desires promotion.

CHAMPAGNE:

Count on me.

BAILIFF:

Or even a simple increase in honorariums.

CHAMPAGNE:

If I am pleased with you—don't say any more—I am going to the port to hire a ship. Till later.

BAILIFF:

To the port.

(Opening a door at the right)

This way, sir, this way—you'll get there much quicker—Till later, sir.

CHAMPAGNE:

Think that you will, answer to me with your head for Prince Stanislas of Poland.

(He leaves)

INNKEEPER: (Entering)

Did you ask him for his papers?

BAILIFF:

Such a person! A friend of the friend of the Abbé Dubois, and of the cousin German of the sovereign prince of—of—never mind! If I can achieve this important capture! What glory!

INNKEEPER: (Looking out the window)

Mr. Bailiff, you don't have your headgear on—

BAILIFF:

Because—

INNKEEPER:

If I actually heard while I was there to hear—

BAILIFF:

Ah, you were then to listen, Mr. Célestin.

INNKEEPER:

For your benefit—I could not leave you alone with a stranger. If I heard correctly, it's about two young men and a young girl.

BAILIFF:

Precisely.

INNKEEPER:

Then that's them—In the court—here!

BAILIFF: (At the window)

Indeed—That's them—Which one is the Prince? Let them come up, Mr. Célestin—keep a watch on them. You'll answer to me for them with your head. So—go—first on foot the Pike-men of the village. Go, Célestin—This is the most beautiful day of my life!

INNKEEPER:

Here they are.

ANDRÉ: (Off in the wings)

We'll rest now until high tide.—See to it the room of our companion be quite well locked and not disturbed. He needs rest.

INNKEEPER:

There's only two of them.

BAILIFF:

Go, Célestin—there's still time. Go arrest the third one.

INNKEEPER:

Yes, Mr. Bailiff.

(He leaves)

MINON: (Falling into a chair)

When I think about my sister, I wish I were dead—

ANDRÉ: Minon, it breaks my heart to see you sad and discouraged—but I love you so much!—To see you cry endlessly.

MINON:

André, you protest the purity of your intentions. I want to believe you—but you haven't yet explained to me.

ANDRÉ:

The presence of the Prince.

MINON:

But at present we are alone.

ANDRÉ:

Some words will suffice to justify my actions.

BAILIFF: (Coming closer)

These an evidently two creatures of the most dangerous type.

ANDRÉ: (Noticing him)

What's this man want?

BAILIFF:

Sir, I have the honor of being the Bailiff of the city of Quilleboeuf.

ANDRÉ:

Sir—

BAILIFF:

Your accomplice's business is over.

ANDRÉ:

What are you saying? Our accomplice?

BAILIFF:

I have the reputation, sir, of being a man who is sober, energetic, and intelligent. I arrest you in the name of the King.

ANDRÉ:

This is a mistake.

BAILIFF:

As well as this young woman.

ANDRÉ:

I am a gentleman, sir.

BAILIFF:

Sir, I'm bailiff, my pike-men are all under arms—all resistance is impossible.

(The innkeeper arrives breathless)

INNKEEPER:

Quick! Quick! There they are!

BAILIFF:

Calm down, Célestin. Of whom are you speaking?

INNKEEPER:

The man who has twenty-eight counting houses or vessels—of sugar cane—and his wife, the Countess—they are here—

ANDRÉ: (Aside)

Cornil—we are lost.

BAILIFF:

Don't say another word, Célestin. I understand—what have you done with the Prince?

INNKEEPER:

In prison?

BAILIFF:

Let these join him. Young man, and you, young lady. Follow this functionary—

(A pike-man enters)

MINON: (To ANDRÉ)

If you resist—you'll be separated from the Prince—

ANDRÉ: (To Bailiff)

We are ready.

BAILIFF:

Go, pike-man—let your companions keep a sharp lookout. Go!

(They leave ROSLAIE and BONAVENTURE enter)

BAILIFF: (Confused and bowing)

Milord and you, Madame—Bow, Célestin.

INNKEEPER:

Milord.

ROSALIE: (Abruptly)

That's fine.

(She walks by) Are they making fun of me?

BONAVENTURE:

The way they're looking at us.

BAILIFF: (To innkeeper)

Célestin?

INNKEEPER:

Milord Bailiff.

BAILIFF:

How odd they are, these foreigners—always incognito. But we aren't taken in by it.

INNKEEPER:

Oh—not at all.

BONAVENTURE:

They are whispering—not a good sign.

ROSALIE: (Low)

We must keep cool.

(Aloud, abruptly) Which of you is the innkeeper?

INNKEEPER:

I am, Madame.

ROSALIE:

Have you already received travelers this morning?

BAILIFF: (Coming forward)

If it pleases your ladyship—

ROSALIE:

No one's talking to you.

BONAVENTURE: (Aside)

The way she treats them.

BAILIFF:

Pardon me if I insist.

(Mysteriously) I know everything.

BONAVENTURE:

He knows everything!

ROSALIE:

What do you know?

BAILIFF:

Everything, Madame Countess.

ROSALIE:

Huh! Madame Countess!

BONAVENTURE:

He said Madame Countess.

BAILIFF:

And you can, therefore, give me orders. You are certain of being obeyed.

ROSALIE:

Orders! Obeyed!

BAILIFF:

Keep your incognitos or not, illustrious lord and powerful lady, in my capacity as Bailiff of Quilleboeuf, the ancient Henricopolis, capital of Remois, allow me to offer you my pure and sincere homage.

INNKEEPER:

And allow me to join in that.

BAILIFF:

Less talk, Célestin—The great do not like long harangues.

(To BONAVENTURE) They are in our power.

BONAVENTURE:

Tell that to the Boss-Lady.

BAILIFF: (Astonished)

The Boss-Lady. (Delighted) Right! Right! That's the Dutch way.

(To ROSALIE) They are in our power.

ROSALIE:

Who's that?

BAILIFF:

Eh, why—the fugitives. We've executed the orders of this high personage—your right arm who is at the port right this moment to charter the ship which is to take Prince Stanislas dead or alive.

ROSALIE: (Aside)

Champagne!

(To BONAVENTURE) I grasp everything—They are talking us for the Dutchman and his wife.

BONAVENTURE:

Not possible.

ROSALIE: (To Bailiff)

What have you done with the fugitives?

BAILIFF:

In prison.

ROSALIE:

Where's the prison?

BAILIFF:

Right here, Madame Countess.

ROSALIE:

What do you mean? Here, in this hotel?

BAILIFF: (To BONAVENTURE)

Milord is an Antiquarian.

BONAVENTURE:

Hell? What? What am I?

ROSALIE:

Indeed, if you please—and don't concern yourself about milord—

BAILIFF: (Aside)

This man doesn't seem like a tyrant!

(Aloud) Madame Countess, the Citadel of Quilleboeuf was erected exactly where we stand—it's a historic, curious fact, and it gives a certain color to the Black Head Inn. There remains a tower in good repair which we rent to Célestin—Célestin is the innkeeper—to use as municipal prison. If by her credit at the court, could you obtain some funds for us to build a more suitable prison....

ROSALIE:

We'll see about it. Is there a well-locked cell in your prison?

BAILIFF:

There's an admirable one, as in ancient times.

ROSALIE:

Suppose someone wanted to get in from outside?

BAILIFF:

To free the prisoners? Impossible. There are these good old bolts—once one has given a twist of the key, it would require a cannon to break down the door.

ROSALIE:

That's fine.

BONAVENTURE: (Aside)

Does she have a cannon?

ROSALIE:

You have some Police in this town?

BAILIFF:

Six veterans and a brigadier.

ROSALIE:

Where are they holed up?

BAILIFF:

At the other end of the street.

ROSALIE:

Call—and have them bring the young girl into my presence with the prisoner called André.

BAILIFF:

Madame Countess, I'm going to find them for you myself.

ROSALIE:

Mr. Bailiff, your zeal will be rewarded. Listen carefully to my instructions—You are going to lock the other prisoner, Prince Stanislas, in that good and solid cell you were telling me about.

BAILIFF:

Yes, Madame Countess.

ROSALIE:

You will bring me the key to it—or better yet—I will go lock the door myself.

BAILIFF: (Aside)

A cautious woman.

(Aloud) If Madame Countess would like to go down to the prison, here's the door to the stairs.

(Pointing to the door at the right)

I'm going to go find the prisoners.

ROSALIE:

Go—and let no one disturb us.

(To BONAVENTURE) But, say something, will you!

BONAVENTURE:

Go—and let no one disturb us.

BAILIFF: (Aside)

The illustrious lord has deigned to open his mouth.

(To innkeeper) Precede me, Célestin—

(He leaves)

ROSALIE:

So, Bonaventure, I have the manner of a Countess?

BONAVENTURE:

You! Ah! Boss-Lady! When you want to—you have the air of a queen.

ROSALIE:

Come, since they take us for the Dutchman and his wife—let's do it.

BONAVENTURE:

What do you mean? What would you do?

ROSALIE:

Since they insist on obeying us despite ourselves—Let's give orders.

BONAVENTURE:

But this Champagne who's going to return….

ROSALIE:

Exactly—we must be prepared before his return. They're coming. It's our fugitives—it's she, it's my sister!

BONAVENTURE: (Hesitating)

Well—are you still furious with her?

ROSALIE:

Certainly—very furious! Ah, My God—how pale she is!

MINON:

Ah, Sis!

ROSALIE:

Come here!

ANDRÉ:

Allow me to explain to you, Madame.

ROSALIE: (To Minon)

Come here, and tell me, immediately, tell—no, no, hug me! First!—I will scold you later. I didn't doubt you for a single moment.—A minute more and I'd have gone mad.

MINON:

Sis—!

ROSALIE: (Pushing her away gently and striding towards André)

As for you—you are a man! You've played a bad and cowardly role.

MINON: (Rushing forward)

Oh, Sis!

ROSALIE:

Isn't he the one who carried you off? Let him reply.

ANDRÉ:

I'm going to reply, Madame, and you will regret your words. I love Minon—but I know she belongs to you because you've been more than a mother to her. I knew that others had planned to rob you of your dear child.

ROSALIE:

Is it possible?

ANDRÉ:

I heard the plot—I saw gold shining—which was the price of the bargain. My oath commanded me to leave. Minon would have remained defenseless against the man who'd sworn in advance to dishonor her.

ROSALIE:

In every bargain there's a seller and a buyer.

ANDRÉ:

The buyer's name is Cornil, the seller is this Champagne.

ROSALIE:

Infamous!

ANDRÉ:

I gathered all my courage. Because it was necessary to brave the tears of the one I love, I carried her off—Madame, I carried her off to protect her honor and her happiness. I carried her off to deliver her to you pure and unstained—And if you are now in each other's arms, both smiling, both happy—it's because I am neither bad nor cowardly as you said, Madame, and that I've been fortunate in playing my role as a man, my fine and simple role of honest man.

ROSALIE:

What do you say about that, Bonaventure?

BONAVENTURE:

Hell! I say that—.

ROSALIE:

You say that I was wrong, right? I'm wrong every way, it's clear. Holy God—I will save the Prince or lose my life. Time's passing. Do you know something?

ANDRÉ:

Many things. First of all, Champagne has presented the bailiff a counterfeit order from the court, and the bailiff will hang the Prince if he's told to.

ROSALIE:

How do you know that the order is false?

ANDRÉ:

Prince Stanislas of Poland is the guest of France—and in whoever's hands power may be, France will never be dishonored.

ROSALIE:

And Champagne's intention?

ANDRÉ:

I know it and can tell you what it is. On the route—at same short distance from here, we were attacked by two scoundrels of his gang—Morel and Robin. They'd been in the pay of the Prince before. The first was able to flee, but I killed the other one, and he said to me as he died, "It's not a prisoner we sold at the price of two million pounds, it's a cadaver."

MINON:

Ah! My God.

ROSALIE:

Is that the way it is? They don't yet have the body?

ANDRÉ:

Alas, Madame, at the point we're at....

ROSALIE: André de Rieux—you are brave?

ANDRÉ: (Ardently)

If I didn't have my hands tied—If I were free—

ROSALIE:

What would you do if you were free?

ANDRÉ:

I'd run to the shore—I notice here the masts of our sloop which is giving signals of departure—a nice little ship. Fast as a bird. Aboard the sloop are twelve Breton sailors—Twelve devils to be correct, chosen by me—one by one—among our best Breton sailors!—If I were free, I'd go seek my twelve sailors! I will return with them, sabers in hand, pistols at our belt—There'll be thirteen of us. That presages death. By the blood of my father, the dead will be those who attempt to bar our passage.

ROSALIE:

André de Rieux, you are free.

ANDRÉ:

Is it possible?

ROSALIE:

You are free—Go, and do as you said.

ANDRÉ:

But, during my absence—The Prince….

ROSALIE:

I'll answer for the prince for an hour—Does that suffice you?

ANDRÉ:

I'll be back in a half hour.

(He leaves)

ROSALIE: (To BONAVENTURE)

Let that one pass, he's one of us.

(To MINON) This door leads to the prison where the Prince is. I want the key to it. Come, Minon.

BONAVENTURE:

And me, Boss-Lady?

ROSALIE: (To BONAVENTURE)

You to the constabulary. Let everybody be on foot. Go!

(She pushes him out) Go!

BONAVENTURE:

It's a short hop there. Let me pass. I'm one of us.

(He leaves—ROSALIE drags MINON to the door at the right. The Bailiff returns at the back with CHAMPAGNE)

BAILIFF: (Entering by the left)

Come, Milord—you are going to find him here. Goodness! No one's here.

CHAMPAGNE:

No one! You are sure they arrived?

BAILIFF:

What do you mean sure? I had the honor of conversing with the illustrious lordship—who spoke very little and the powerful lady, who, on the contrary, spoke considerably and very well.

CHAMPAGNE: (Aside)

I wanted to get the job done before the arrival of Master Van Zuyp—but since he's here, (Aloud) inform Mynheer Van Zuyp and the Countess of my arrival.

BAILIFF:

Madame Countess. There's a determined woman. She asked for the key to the prison—and I gave the order to deliver it to her.

CHAMPAGNE:

The key to the prison?

BAILIFF:

In which she had the Prince locked up—

CHAMPAGNE:

The Countess! Now that's very odd!

BAILIFF:

Ah, ah—she wanted to know if the door was good—and now that she has that key, the devil himself won't get near the prisoner. As for the illustrious lordship—

CHAMPAGNE:

I'll wait for them here—Go!

BAILIFF:

I'll bring them to you right away—

CHAMPAGNE: (Alone)

Everything's ready. The ship's waiting. True God—I will combat hell to get this fortune. Luckily (he laughs), it isn't necessary to deploy so much courage. The Countess has the key to the prison. She'll give it to me. I will find a pretext to manage all alone—the embarking of the Prince—and once at sea (he takes one of his pistols in hand). The charge—is worth exactly a million roubles. Someone's coming.

(He hides his pistol) It's the step of a woman.—The Countess, no doubt.

(ROSALIE enters by the door at the right)

That woman here.

(He recoils)

ROSALIE:

It's a veritable fortress.

(Noticing CHAMPAGNE)

Has he seen this key?

CHAMPAGNE: (Aside)

The battle's not yet over.

ROSALIE: (Aside)

I have to keep him for twenty minutes.

(Aloud) It seems we are destined to meet always and everywhere, Mr. Champagne.

CHAMPAGNE:

I wasn't looking for you.

ROSALIE:

As for me, I was seeking you.

CHAMPAGNE:

Why would you seek me?

ROSALIE:

To tell you that you lied. The Prince didn't carry off my young sister. It was you who wanted to carry her off to sell her to your Master.

CHAMPAGNE: (Aside)

If Mynheer Van Zuyp and the Countess were in this hotel, they'd have come already.

(Aloud) Yes, I did have that notion, Madame Valentin.

ROSALIE:

You don't even attempt to deny it?

CHAMPAGNE: (Aside, absorbed)

The Countess wouldn't have asked for the key to the prison.

(Heading toward the door at the back) We are going to chat about that, Madame Valentin—and so as not to be disturbed.... (He locks the door at the back)

ROSALIE: (Aside)

Time's passing—every minute that he loses—

(Aloud) Lock it, Mr. Champagne, lock it as much as you wish.

CHAMPAGNE: (Going to lock the door at the left, aside)

But where is Bonaventure?

(Aloud, and pointing to the small door at the right) I'm not locking that one.

ROSALIE: (Shivering)

Because—

CHAMPAGNE:

Because that one leads to the Prison of the Prince.

ROSALIE:

I don't know.

CHAMPAGNE: (Stopping before her)

You don't know? Is that the truth?

ROSALIE:

How would I know?

CHAMPAGNE:

You are severe towards those who lie—still—To what door is the key you were holding on to when you entered?

ROSALIE:

What key?

CHAMPAGNE:

Show it to me.

ROSALIE:

I don't have any key.

CHAMPAGNE:

Madame Valentin—you are young, strong, courageous, you are beautiful, you are happy. You cling to life, I'm sure of it.

ROSALIE:

It's true, I cling to it.

CHAMPAGNE:

Why are you gambling with it?

ROSALIE:

Me, gamble with my life? Come off it.

CHAMPAGNE:

It's useless to feign. You want to save the young Prince. To do that you assumed the name of the Countess. I had raised her because of the need of our interests to a pedestal. You climbed up on that pedestal—you found people excessively credulous, you profited by it—As you knew my plan, you placed the Prince in the shelter of a strong prison, and for greater security you are carrying the key yourself—I want that key—give it to me.

ROSALIE:

No.

CHAMPAGNE:

Madame Valentin, you love money above all else.

ROSALIE:

They accuse me of that.

CHAMPAGNE:

Give me that key.

ROSALIE:

No.

CHAMPAGNE:

I'll buy it from you—for 50,000 pounds—double that—half a million.

ROSALIE:

No.

CHAMPAGNE:

A whole million.

ROSALIE:

I told you no.

CHAMPAGNE: (Catching her glancing at the window)

You're waiting for help.

ROSALIE:

Yes!

CHAMPAGNE:

Listen, woman—I have nothing against you, but I need this fortune. Give me the key or I'll kill you.

(ROSALIE puts her hand to her breast)

(Aside) That's where the key is—! At last!

(Pulling her empty hand out, aside) No, no—I won't use that weapon.

(Aloud) I'm not afraid. Does one kill a woman?

CHAMPAGNE:

In that case, you don't know me. Because you reply to me, "One doesn't kill a woman." You are deceived by my attire—you take me for a gentleman! Lady, I'm a valet—a valet, you understand—a lackey, a scoundrel—and for gold—Ah, you are really going to find out; for gold—as for me, I'm capable of killing women. The key is there—in your bosom—give it to me.

ROSALIE: (Hand on her breast)

No.

(Aside) If I was a man....

CHAMPAGNE:

Give me that key or I'll kill you.

ROSALIE: (Aside)

I'm only a woman—I feel the courage to die—I don't feel the courage to kill.

CHAMPAGNE: (Aside)

The noise of gunfire would ruin me—and I don't have a dagger.

(Aloud) Hear me further and you won't resist any more. You are going to see that I am capable of killing a woman. One day I found myself face to face with an old geezer that illness and age nailed to his bed. When I noticed his thin and emaciated face surrounded by white hair, and his breast that raised a panting breath, I hesitated, as I hesitate today—woman! Not long, perhaps.

(He grabs ROSALIE's arm; she listens motionless and avidly)

Because today it's a question of two million pounds, and the old geezer had only 700 crowns in his mattress.

ROSALIE: (Standing up and grabbing him)

Ah! It's you who killed my father!

(They struggle. CHAMPAGNE succeeds in disengaging his hand which holds a pistol. ROSALIE pulls a pistol from her breast and blows his brains out—The door at the rear is forced in and gives way. Great tumult. ANDRE leaps through the window followed by his Breton sailors. BONAVENTURE, MINON and CORNIL also enter through the door, which is forced open)

ANDRÉ: (Rushing forward)

She didn't need us!

ROSALIE:

He was the murderer of my father.

(They pick up CHAMPAGNE)

BONAVENTURE:

And I didn't want her to take her pistols!

ROSALIE: (Giving him the key to the prison)

Go, free the Prince!

(To Bailiff who enters, pointing to CORNIL) Arrest that man!

CORNIL:

By what right?

BAILIFF:

I obey Madame Countess of Pfaffenhoffen—

CORNIL:

My wife—Where the devil is she?

BAILIFF:

Let him be seized, let him be taken away.

ROSALIE: (To CORNIL)

If there's a criminal indictment, witnesses won't be lacking. The justice of France will decide your fate!

(To STANISLAS, who enters with BONAVENTURE) Prince, you are free.

A SAILOR: The tide won't wait. On board, on board!

STANISLAS:

Children, friends, may God give you happiness! Miss, lucky or unlucky, I shall never forget that I owe you my life.

BONAVENTURE:

Ah—Boss-Lady!—If you knew....

ROSALIE:

I know—Now, I know, my lad—here, take my hand.

BONAVENTURE:

Your hand! I will be the husband of the Boss-Lady.

ALL: Goodbye! Goodbye!

CURTAIN

ABOUT FRANK J. MORLOCK

FRANK J. MORLOCK has written and translated many plays since retiring from the legal profession in 1992. His translations have also appeared on Project Gutenberg, the Alexandre Dumas Père web page, Literature in the Age of Napoléon, Infinite Artistries.com, and Munsey's (formerly Blackmask). In 2006 he received an award from the North American Jules Verne Society for his translations of Verne's plays. He lives and works in México.

www.ingramcontent.com/pod-product-compliance
Lightning Source LLC
LaVergne TN
LVHW040116080426
835507LV00039B/389